D0882892

GULLS : A GUIDE TO IDENTIFICATION

GULLS

A Guide to Identification

by P. J. GRANT

Illustrated by the author

BUTEO BOOKS
Vermillion, South Dakota

Library of Congress Catalog Card No. 81–71625
ISBN 0–931130–08–5

Published in USA 1982 by Buteo Books,
PO Box 481, Vermillion, South Dakota 57069 and
in Great Britain by T & A D Poyser Ltd,
Town Head House, Calton, Waterhouses, Staffordshire, England

This book is based largely on material which first
appeared in the Journal British Birds Vols 71–74, 1978–81

Text set in 9/10½ pt Linotron 202 Plantin,
printed and bound at The Pitman Press, Bath

Contents

Photographs

Introduction

Gulls are widely abundant; they are relatively large, comparatively approachable, and are often slow-flying. They thus provide ample opportunity for close study, unequalled by other groups of birds. It is possible to observe the timing and progress of their moults, the effects of wear and fading on their plumage, and the changes in appearance brought about by these factors. The topography of their plumage can be closely studied, and the various groups of feathers and their arrangement in different postures can be distinguished. Distance and changed light conditions affect their colour tones, and partly subjective criteria such as size, structure and flight action are important in their identification. They are prone to hybridity and plumage abnormalities such as leucism and albinism. In fact, they demonstrate an almost complete range of factors which, with proper interpretation, are relevant to the identification of most other birds. Competence in identifying and ageing gulls can provide an invaluable foundation for competence in bird identification generally. I recommend gull-watching to beginner and expert birdwatcher alike: gulls provide a test-bed for identification skills at all levels of experience.

However, standard field guides do not adequately cover the complexities of identifying and ageing gulls. This situation prompted the publication of a series of five papers dealing with the field identification of west Palearctic gulls in the monthly journal *British Birds* (71: 145–176; 72: 142–182; 73: 113–158; 74: 111–142 and 74: 363–394). This book is an enlarged and much revised version of those papers, with many new and additional photographs: it deals with the 23 species of gulls (about half the world total) which occur in Europe, the Middle East, and eastern North America.

The ability to recognise the age of an individual immature is just as important as specific identification. It is a challenge in its own right to the serious bird-identifier, but it is also of value in studies of population, distribution and migration. Indeed, identification and ageing go hand-in-hand, for it is only by practising his skills on common species—of all ages—that an observer will acquire the degree of familiarity necessary for the confident identification of the occasional rarity.

Suggested amendments to the text, illustrations or maps, or new photographs, would be welcomed for possible inclusion in future editions of this book. They should be sent to P. J Grant, 14 Heathfield Road, Ashford, Kent TN24 8QD, or c/o T. & A. D. Poyser Ltd.

Acknowledgements

The large and enthusiastic response to appeals for information and photographs for this project has made this book much more complete than would otherwise have been the case, and I am greatly indebted to all those who have contributed.

The photographs published here are a selected fraction of those received, which in total have provided an invaluable source of reference. I am particularly grateful to Dr Richard Chandler, M. D. Gallagher, Peter M. Harris, Dr Pamela Harrison, E. J. Mackrill and Norman van Swelm, who provided an exceptional number of photographs, taken mostly with this project especially in mind: EJM's expertly analysed field notes and priceless portraits of Franklin's Gull from breeding and wintering areas prompted extensive revisions of the original text for that species, and provided confirmation of its atypical moults which have previously not been fully described. Jeffery Boswall, R. A. Hume and Bernard King have been regular correspondents, supplying many useful leads and much literature and information. Gull skins at the British Museum (Natural History), Tring, have been an essential reference: I thank the staff for their ready assistance during my frequent visits. Descriptions of rare gulls on the files of the *British Birds* Rarities Committee have been a most useful reference: I thank the observers who submitted them and Michael J. Rogers, the Committee's secretary, for making them available to me.

I thank I. J. Ferguson-Lees, P. F. Bonham and the other members of the *British Birds* editorial board for much constructive criticism and advice during the initial planning of the series of papers in that journal, especially the present managing editor Dr J. T. R. Sharrock for his substantial encouragement and assistance during its preparation and publication. I am especially grateful to H. A. R. Cawkell who, by his sound advice, started my interest in gulls, and to R. E. Scott from whose expertise I greatly benefited during my initial studies of gull plumages.

The enormous debt owed to Jonathan Dwight and his classic monograph *The Gulls of the World* (1925) is readily acknowledged: his work remains an essential reference for gull enthusiasts after more than half a century.

For their provision of photographs, information, advice, opinions, criticisms and various assistance, I sincerely thank the following:
F. G. H. Allen, R. Allison, T. B. Ardamatskaya, Keith Atkin, S. Baines, D. Banks, R. Barber, John Barlee, Bengt Bengtsson, Arnoud B. van den Berg, R. Bijlsma, T. E. Bond, J. B. & S. Bottomley, Dr W. R. P. Bourne, T. E. Bowley, Alan Brady, E. A. Bragin, D. J. Britton, P. L. Britton, A. Brown, R. Burridge, G. P. Catley, P. Chadder, M. L. Chalmers, S. Chapman, John W. Chardine, J. Charman, R. A. Cheke, C. Clark, William S. Clark, J. R. Clarkson, B. M. Clarkson, J. Chardine, R. H. Charlwood, P. Clement, D. L. Clugston, M. Coath, R. K. Coles, S. G. D Cook, R. Coomber, D. M. Cottridge, Dennis Coutts, Stanley Cramp, J. G. Cranfield, A. J. Croucher, L. J. Davenport, M. Davenport, M. Davies, N. R. Davies, G. Davis, Tom Davis, A. R. Dean, I. Dawson, M. Densley, Dr P. Devillers, Wendy Dickson, F. Dixon, P. A. Doherty, G. van Duin, Jon Dunn, P. J. Dunn, J. N. Dymond, J. Elmelid, F. Erhardt, D. Emley, Davis Finch, Crispin Fisher, G. H. Fisher, P. R. Flint, A. Forsyth, T. Francis, R. Frankum, R. A. Frost, R. Frost, J. R. Furse, E. F. J. Garcia, Frank B. Gill, Dr Peter Gloe, P. D. Goriup, M. Gosselin, P. Grandjean,

12 Acknowledgements

P. J. Greenhalf, A. J. Greenland, P. Gregory, Harold E. Grenfell, J. Haapala, S. Hahn, D. M. Hanford, M. Hario, Dr M. P. Harris, S. Harris, W. G. Harvey, D. M. Hawker, Brian Hawkes, P. de Heer, Stellan Hedgren, P. Helo, R. Higson, W. R. Hirst, R. N. Hobbs, R. H. Hogg, A. J. Holcombe, M. A. Hollingworth, S. Holohan, R. A. Hughes, B. Hulbert, D. B. Hunt, E. J. van IJzendoorn, V. Iljashenko, T. P. Inskipp, H. Insley, Eric Isakson, F. H. Jansen, J. V. Jenson, E. de Juana, T. Källqvist, A. Keppler, Jan Kihlman, P. K. Kinnear, J. Kist, A. A. Kistchinski, Alan Kitson, P. de Knijff, A. J. Knystautas, Dr Brigitte Königstedt, Dr D. Königstedt, A. F. Kovshaz, J. van der Laan, Lars Larsson, L. A. Laidler, Lasse J. Laine, C. S. Lawson, Paul Lehman, C. R. Linfoot, L. Lippens, S. C. Madge, W. & I. Makatsch, P. Maker, K. K. Malmström, E. L. Marchant, B. A. Marsh, E. Maugham, N. V. McCanch, A. McGeehan, B. S. Meadows, Piet Meeth, H. Meltofte, Kauri Mikkola, T. Milbled, J. Miller, Richard T. Mills, F. de Miranda, D. Moerbeek, Dr P. Monaghan, S. Moon, C. C. Moore, S. Mori, J. Moss, Killian Mullarney, Wim C. Mullié, Dr Irene Neufeldt, Gerry Nicholls, J. C. Nicholls, P. F. Nichols, P. Nicolau-Guillaumet, D. M. Norman, P. Oliver, Gerald J. Oreel, G. L. Ouweneel, M. J. Palmer, J. Palmgren, E. N. Panov, M. Parker, T. Parmenter, K. Pellow, P. Perry, T. Pettay, U. Pfaendler, Jeff Pick, René Pop, Richard Porter, Peter W. Post, A. J. Prater, E. S. & S. R. D. da Prato, J. G. Prins, P. Puhjo, Dr M. N. Rankin, V. Ree, G. H. Rees, J. F. Reynolds, P. Richardson, J. De Ridder, A. H. Rider, Don Roberson, A. Roberts, N. Rogers, S. Rooke, Will Russell, J. Seeviour, T. Shiota, J. C. Sinclair, M. Sinden, V. D. Siokhin, H. B. Skjelstad, D. Smallshire, Donald A. Smith, P. William Smith, R. Smith, J. B. Steeves, P. Steyn, E. Stirling, Ralph Stokoe, P. J. Strangeman, M. P. Sutherland, Lars Svensson, M. E. Taylor, Jean Terschuren, D. Thomas, P. Tomkovitch, Gerald Tuck, N. Tucker, Laurel A. Tucker, V. Tucker, Bobby Tulloch, R. E. Turley, David & Katie Urry, J. van Impe, J. M. Varela, Richard Vaughan, P. Vines, K. E. Vinicombe, E. de Visser, J. Visser, M. A. Voinstvensky, Prof. Dr K. H. Voous, D. I. M. Wallace, F. E. Warr, A. Wassink, C. E. Wheeler, A. Williams, Ian Willis, M. B. Withers, P. Yésou, B. Zonfrillo, V. A. Zubakin and L. Zykova.

General Information

A thorough understanding of the following general aspects of gull plumage will greatly clarify the seemingly complex field situation, and will provide the essential foundation for expertise in identifying and ageing gulls.

LENGTH OF IMMATURITY

The length of time taken for a gull to reach adult plumage is generally related to the size of the species—the smaller the gull, the shorter its period of immaturity. Most small species (e.g. Black-headed Gull) become indistinguishable from the adult with the full acquisition of second-winter plumage (about 13–16 months after hatching), most medium-sized species (e.g. Common Gull) with third-winter plumage (about 25-28 months after hatching), and most large species (e.g. Herring Gull) with fourth-winter plumage (about 37–40 months after hatching). Fig. 1. shows the timing of moults and the sequence of plumages, from juvenile to adult, of typical small, medium-sized and large gulls. There are exceptions to this general rule; probably the majority of Little Gulls, for example, have readily distinguishable second-year plumages, and do not become fully adult until third-winter plumage is acquired (instead of second-winter as might be expected in view of the species' very small size). This and other exceptions and variations are fully described in the respective species accounts.

AGE TERMINOLOGY

Use of the age terminology used in Fig. 1 is recommended when describing the age of an individual gull. It avoids the imprecision of such terms as 'immature' or 'sub-adult', which are unhelpfully used to describe individual gulls in many field guides and in records submitted to local bird reports. Even 'first-*year*' (instead of the more precise 'first-winter' or 'first-summer'), 'second-*year*' and so on are inadequate in late summer or autumn, since they do not indicate whether the individual has undertaken its autumn moult and, therefore, do not indicate whether it is at the beginning or end of its 'year'. When a gull is in a transitional stage of moult, it is useful to record this fact, e.g. 'first-summer moulting to second-winter'. In some cases, especially with immatures of the large species (as explained more fully in the introduction to group three) it may not be possible to age individuals more precisely than, for example, 'second- or third-summer': in cases where the differences between winter and summer plumage are not well-marked, it may not even be possible to get closer than 'second- or third-year' or 'first-winter or -summer', although whether it is a summer or winter plumage will often be obvious, of course, from the month of observation.

The more general terms 'first-year' (referring to juvenile, first-winter and first-summer plumages together), 'second-year' (second-winter and second-summer), 'third-year' (third-winter and third-summer) and so on, may be used when referring to the general age groups of gulls. This 'plumage-year' terminology should not be confused with 'calendar-year' terminology i.e. 'first calendar-year' (referring to individuals from fledging to 31st December of their hatching year), 'second calendar-year' (1st January to 31st December of the year after hatching) and so on. Use of calendar-year terminology is appropriate whenever precise plumage definition is unnecessary. Euring codes, used by ringers, are 3J (juvenile), 3 (first calendar-year, not juvenile), 5 (second calendar-year), 7 (third calendar-year) and so on (thus odd numbers for individuals of known age); and 2 (age unknown), 4 (at least second calendar-year), 6 (at least third calendar-year) and so on (thus even numbers for individuals for which the hatching year cannot be determined). The term 'immature' refers to individuals in any plumage other than adult. Gulls occasionally breed in the immature summer plumage of the year prior to that in which they first acquire full adult summer plumage.

MOULT

The first moult of all gulls is the post-juvenile moult to first-winter plumage, which commences at or shortly after fledging. It is a partial moult, replacing the juvenile head and body feathers, and also an individually variable amount of coverts of the inner wing, reducing the extent of the dark carpal-bar of many small and medium-sized species. Subsequently, there is a regular sequence at all ages of two moults a year—a partial one in spring, and a complete one in autumn.

Spring moult: this is a partial moult replacing the head and body feathers, resulting in immature or adult summer plumage. On small and medium-sized species, this moult often also includes some or, rarely, most of the coverts of the inner wing (further reducing the extent of the carpal-bar), sometimes the tertials, and (especially on Little Gull, but also occasionally on some other small species) one or more pairs of central tail feathers (rarely the whole tail), causing a white gap in the otherwise complete dark tail band of first-summers.

Autumn moult: this is a complete moult, resulting in immature or adult winter plumage. Adults usually start the moult near the end of breeding activity; immatures begin the moult earlier. Large species can take as long as four or five months to complete this moult, whereas small species take four to six weeks, but there is much individual variation both in the duration of the moult and in the starting time. Some immature large gulls may start the moult as early as May, while some adults may not complete it until December or January. The moult dates given in the species accounts refer to the extreme dates between which active moult can be expected: most individuals will start and complete their moult within this period.

Broadly speaking, the moult of the primaries provides the yardstick by which the progress of the autumn moult is measured. The moult commences with the shedding of the 10th (innermost) primary, and progresses outwards. The moult of the rest of the plumage takes place mainly within the period when the primaries are being renewed, so that the full growth of the 1st (outermost) primary comes at or near the end of the moult. The rate of renewal of the primaries is slow, with usually only two or three adjacent feathers growing at any one time.

The secondaries and tail feathers are moulted in a much less regular pattern, and large gaps are often visible where groups of feathers have been shed simultaneously. Wing coverts are shed in groups, revealing the whitish bases of the underlying

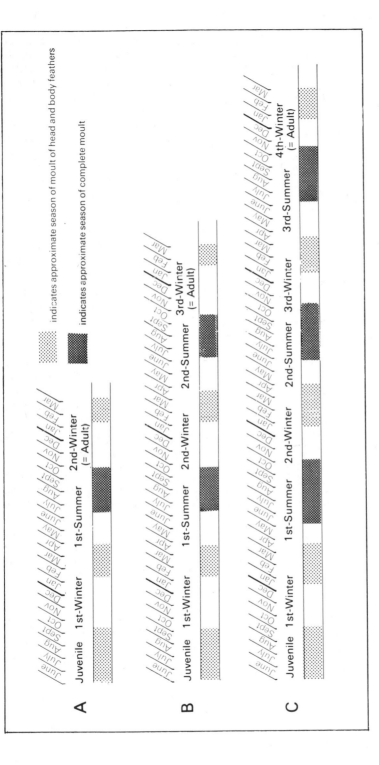

Fig. 1. Sequence of plumages and moults from juvenile to adult of typical small (A), medium (B) and large (C) gulls.

feathers, producing whitish patches and lines on the upperwing in late summer and autumn, which are especially obvious on adults of species with a dark grey or blackish upperwing.

Exceptions: two species covered in this book are exceptions to these general rules about the timing and extent of the spring and autumn moults. Sabine's Gull has a complete moult in spring, and a partial one in autumn (the reverse of the moult timing in other gulls), and juvenile plumage is retained throughout the first autumn, the post-juvenile moult not beginning until after arrival in the wintering areas. Franklin's Gull has the usual post-juvenile moult, but subsequently has a complete moult in spring and another in autumn. The timing and extent of the moults of these two species are more fully discussed in the respective species accounts.

Miscellaneous: the outer primaries and tail feathers of juvenile gulls, which are retained throughout the first year, are rather pointed and rounded respectively. At subsequent ages (second-winter onwards), the outer primaries have more rounded tips and the tail feathers are square-ended. Although these differences are rarely discernible in the field, they are sometimes a useful clue to age in sharp photographs.

When a feather is lost accidentally, its replacement usually resembles that which would normally have grown at the next moult. Immatures with one or more replacement tail feathers are quite frequent, showing as a white break in the otherwise complete tail band.

Sick or injured adult gulls which are unable to return to the breeding colony, or are unable to participate in colonial breeding activity, may lack the stimulus which produces summer plumage.

WEAR AND FADING

The effects of wear and fading are always most obvious in the summer, when the wing and tail feathers are at their oldest, just before the complete autumn moult. White plumage is more prone to wear than dark, and the white tips and fringes may disappear completely. Brown plumage, especially the wing coverts of immatures, fades markedly with age, often to whitish; and black or blackish areas progressively fade browner.

By late summer or early autumn, when the wing and tail moult is under way, the mixture of faded and worn old feathers and complete and growing new ones often presents a most bedraggled appearance, especially on immatures, and produces wing patterns which may be unfamiliar. Further, while the outermost primaries are still growing, the wing-tip is more blunt or rounded than normal, and the wing-beat is quicker than usual until the full extent of the wing area is restored. It is impossible to illustrate the endless variations of wing pattern exhibited by gulls in wing moult, but their appearance can be visualised by comparing the wing patterns of the two adjacent ages involved. As an example, Fig. 2 shows some transitional wing patterns of a typical Mediterranean Gull moulting from first-summer to second-winter.

SEXING

Males are generally larger than females, with larger bills. There are few, if any, reliable differences as to plumage or bare parts coloration. So sexing gulls in the field is, at least, difficult. The structural differences can often be discerned, however, in a

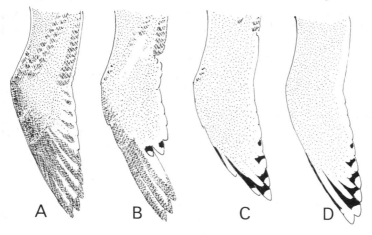

Fig. 2.   Wing of **Mediterranean Gull** *Larus melanocephalus* in moult from first-summer to second-winter. (A) faded first-summer pattern immediately prior to start of moult; (B) moult half complete, inner four primaries new, 5th and 6th partially grown, 4th missing, 1st–3rd old; outer secondaries new, and white patches on inner wing indicating moult of coverts; (C) moult three-quarters complete, 1st and 2nd partially grown and held partially concealed by adjacent primaries; note that tips of outer primaries rounded in second-year (and subsequently), not pointed as in first-year; (D) fresh second-winter pattern.

pair standing side-by-side, or alternatively sex can be determined by behaviour in breeding areas. The size differences between sexes are generally more marked in the larger species.

FORMAT

Each of the five groups brings together species which share similar characters, especially in their immature plumages where the possibility of confusion is greatest. The introduction to each group covers general points relating to the species which it includes, with a table of measurements from Dwight (1925) and a page of drawings depicting standing birds in first-winter plumage to aid size and structure comparisons. Dwight's measurements are included because they are a readily obtainable series by the same measurer and because they provide an indication of the size variation within each species, and to aid size comparisons between different species for field purposes: in some cases the samples are small, and thus probably do not indicate the extremes of variation.

The wing measurements were taken with the wing in its natural position, not with primaries straightened and flattened as is the modern practice: Dwight calculated that measurements taken by the latter method would produce results on large wings averaging 2.3% greater, and on smaller wings averaging 1.9% greater. Bill measurement is from the tip to the forwardmost extension of feathering on the culmen.

The general introduction is followed by the species accounts, including flight drawings of adults and immatures of each species (in which the wing length and tail spreads have been slightly exaggerated to enable the flight patterns to be more clearly shown), a map showing world distribution, an identification summary, an ageing summary (intended as a quick reference to the main age characters of each species), detailed descriptions of each plumage from juvenile to adult, and (in the cases of Herring and Lesser Black-backed Gulls) a section on geographical variation in which the differences between subspecies are described.

The photographs have been selected to illustrate the identification features of as many different plumages as possible for each species.

TOPOGRAPHY

Topographical terminology follows that recommended by *British Birds* magazine (74: 239–242), with the addition of several terms applicable to special plumage features of gulls, marked * in the charts.

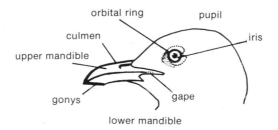

Head—bare parts
The orbital ring is the fleshy, unfeathered (and, on adult gulls, often brightly coloured) ring immediately surrounding the eye. The *mouth* is the fleshy interior of the bill.

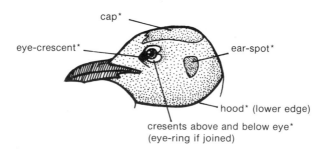

Head—plumage marks

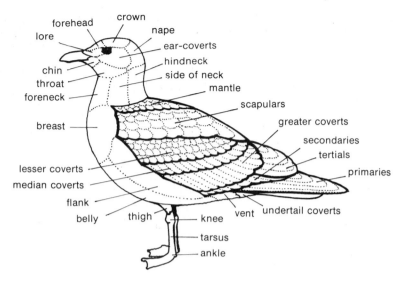

Standing gull

More or less of the coverts of the inner wing will be visible depending on the extent to which the scapulars are held bunched or spread: often, most of the coverts will be concealed by the overlapping scapulars and breast-side and flank feathers so that, for example, the carpal-bar of many first-year gulls will be totally invisible on a standing bird. The *scapular-crescent*★ (formed by white tips to the rearmost scapulars) and *tertial-crescent*★ (formed by white tips of the longest tertials) are often prominent on standing gulls of some species, contrasting with the otherwise grey or blackish coloration of the remainder of their upperparts.

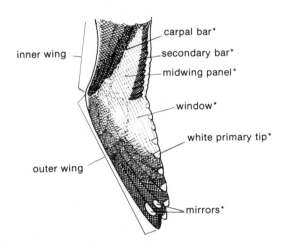

Wing markings

The mirrors are usually not visible on the closed wing (unless it is spread when preening, or unless the wing-tip can be viewed from below): they should not be confused with the white primary tips which are always visible on a perched gull.

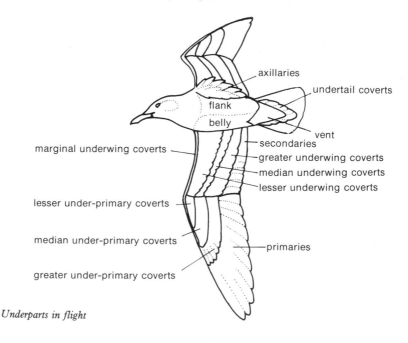

scapulars

back

mantle

rump

marginal coverts

uppertail coverts

lesser coverts

median coverts

greater coverts

lesser primary coverts

10th   secondaries

9th

alula

8th

7th

median primary coverts

6th

5th

greater primary coverts

4th

3rd

primaries
(numbered inwards)

2nd

1st

Upperparts in flight

Gulls have eleven primaries, but the vestigial outermost one is ignored here; in this book
the primaries are numbered inwards from the outermost large (1st) primary to the
innermost (10th). Note that the scapulars extend back as the wing is opened, covering the
tertials completely in flight (the white scapular-crescent thus forms the inner part of the
white trailing edge of the inner wing in flight).

axillaries

undertail coverts

flank

belly

vent

marginal underwing coverts

secondaries

greater underwing coverts

median underwing coverts

lesser underwing coverts

lesser under-primary coverts

median under-primary coverts

primaries

greater under-primary coverts

Underparts in flight

Black-headed, Slender-billed,
Bonaparte's and Grey-headed Gulls

These four small- to medium-sized species form a distinct group among western Palearctic gulls. Their most striking common feature is the extensive white on the leading edge of the outer wing in flight. This is more extensive on adults than on immatures, but is readily visible at all ages. It is least extensive on Grey-headed Gull, which also has mirrors on the outer two primaries when adult, giving a diagnostic wing pattern; on this species—unlike the other three—the white leading edge is not visible from below.

Immatures of all four have dusky head markings of varying strength, wing patterns of brownish carpal-bar and blackish secondary bar, as well as the white on the leading edge, and white tails with a thin, clear cut, blackish subterminal band. These characters in combination are not shared by any other western Palearctic gull.

All except Slender-billed have dark hoods in adult summer plumage, but—surprisingly—even that species usually has an ear-spot in winter and immature plumages, although it is much more faint than on the others.

Black-headed, Slender-billed and Bonaparte's normally reach adult plumage in their second winter; some Grey-headeds probably do so as well, but others have identifiable second-year plumages and do not become fully adult until their third winter. The proportion of Grey-headed Gulls having this longer immaturity is not known, but it is clearly much greater than for the others in this group, for which it is rarely possible to distinguish between second-years and adults.

Throughout most of its range, the Black-headed is the commonest and most familiar small gull (Fig. 4). Slender-billed is rare anywhere north of its localised Mediterranean and southwest Asian breeding areas (Fig. 6). Bonaparte's is a rare

Table 1: Measurements (mm) of four gulls Larus *(from Dwight 1925)*

	sample	wing	tail	bill	tarsus
Black-headed Gull *L. ridibundus*	12	280–315	104–124	30–37	42–47
Slender-billed Gull *L. genei*	24	278–320	110–125	35–46	46–54
Bonaparte's Gull *L. philadelphia*	27	246–271	99–108	27–32	33–37
Grey-headed Gull *L. cirrocephalus*	22	305–338	120–134	35–42	48–60

Fig. 3.   First-winter **Black-headed** *Larus ridibundus*, **Slender-billed** *L. genei*, **Bonaparte's** *L. philadelphia* and **Grey-headed Gulls** *L. cirrocephalus*, showing comparative sizes, shapes and stances

vagrant from America (Fig. 8), with only one or two records annually in Britain. Grey-headed is the typical gull of some African coasts and inland lakes (Fig. 10), and has been recorded only once in Europe (Ree 1973).

For European observers, the abundance of the Black-headed Gull makes it the key species for identifying the others in this group. Complete familiarity with its appearance, especially in immature plumages, from different angles and in varying light conditions, will greatly aid recognition of the others, and avoid the dismissal of one of them as an odd-looking Black-headed.

Black-headed Gull
Larus ridibundus

(Figs 3A and 5, Photographs 1–22)

Adult winter

IDENTIFICATION

This is the smallest of the abundant western Palearctic gulls. It is noticeably smaller than the European race of the Common Gull *L. c. canus*, and this is accentuated in flight, when the slimmer, more pointed wings and quicker wingbeats are discernible. It is easily separable from all gulls except the other three species in this group, the best point being the white along the leading edge of the outer wing in flight—more extensive on adults than immatures—visible at long range from both above and below. The brown hood of summer adults and some first-summer birds is diagnostic among western Palearctic gulls (the others having black or grey hoods), but it invariably looks blackish at a distance. In winter, the head is mainly white, with a neat blackish ear-spot and eye-crescent; the bill is maroon-red in breeding plumage, red or bright red with dark tip in winter, and dull flesh or yellowish-flesh with dark tip on first-years. The legs are the same colour as the bill.

The separation of Black-headed from the other three species in this group is less straightforward: the brown hood colour of summer adults is the only wholly diagnostic character, so a combination of factors involving size, structure and plumage must be used. With practice, a quick scan through flocks of Black-headed Gulls—checking characters of size, head pattern and shape, and wing pattern—is sufficient to eliminate the possible presence of one of the other species: Bonaparte's is smaller, with a neat blackish bill and translucent white primaries; Slender-billed has a diagnostically elongated forehead and bill, and head all white or with a very pale grey earspot; Grey-headed is larger and more heavily built, with a wholly dusky underwing and a distinctive wing pattern.

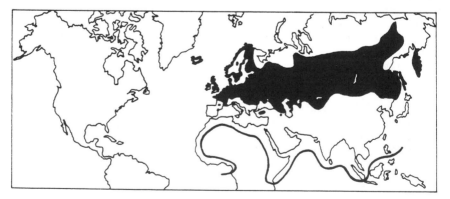

Fig. 4.   World distribution of **Black-headed Gull** *Larus ridibundus*, showing approximate breeding range (solid black) and approximate southern limit of winter/non-breeding range (black line). Has bred Newfoundland, and records in North America increasing.

Juvenile: extensive ginger-brown on head, mantle, scapulars and sides of breast (summer to late September).

First-winter: grey mantle and scapulars, brown carpal-bar, blackish secondary bar and tail band, winter head pattern (July to April).

First-summer: faded pale brown carpal-bar, blackish secondary bar and tail band, hood developed to variable extent (March to October).

Second-winter and second-summer: a very few can be aged as second years (see detailed description under second-winter), but vast majority inseparable from adults.

Adult winter/second-winter: adult wing pattern, all-white-tail, winter head pattern (August to March).

Adult summer/second-summer: adult wing pattern, all-white, fully developed hood (January to October).

DETAILED DESCRIPTIONS

Juvenile (Fig. 5A; underwing and tail similar to first-winter 5F)

HEAD White, washed buff when recently-fledged, with dark markings forming partial hood, separated from mantle by white collar on hindneck.

BODY Underparts and rump mainly white, breast faintly washed buff when recently-fledged. Mantle, scapulars, lower hindneck and breast-sides mainly rich ginger-brown, with pale-fringed feathers giving scaled effect on scapulars.

WINGS Brown carpal-bar; tertials brown, broadly fringed paler. Secondaries blackish with pale fringes, forming subterminal secondary bar. Greater coverts mainly pale grey, forming pale mid-wing panel. Typical outer wing patterns shown in 5A and 5B: exceptionally, black on outer primaries more extensive, reducing white to two elongated mirrors as in 5C. Primaries may have tiny white tips from 3rd inwards. From below, secondaries and outer primaries appear mainly blackish-grey, with narrow translucent white leading edge to outer wing.

TAIL White, with clear-cut narrow subterminal band, broadest in centre, outer pair of feathers sometimes all-white.

BARE PARTS Iris dark brown, basal two-thirds of bill dull flesh or yellowish-flesh, tip blackish; legs dull yellowish-flesh.

First-winter (Figs. 3A, 5B and 5F) Acquired by post-juvenile head and body moult, which starts at fledging and is usually complete by late September.

HEAD White, with dusky eye-crescent and prominent blackish ear-spot.

BODY Mantle and scapulars uniform pale grey, sometimes a few brown juvenile feathers retained. Very pale grey wash extending from mantle to lower hindneck and breast-sides. Rump and underparts white.

WINGS As juvenile, but brown and blackish areas faded paler, and white tips on primaries and secondaries reduced or lacking.

TAIL As juvenile, but band faded, and terminal whitish fringe reduced.

BARE PARTS Much as juvenile.

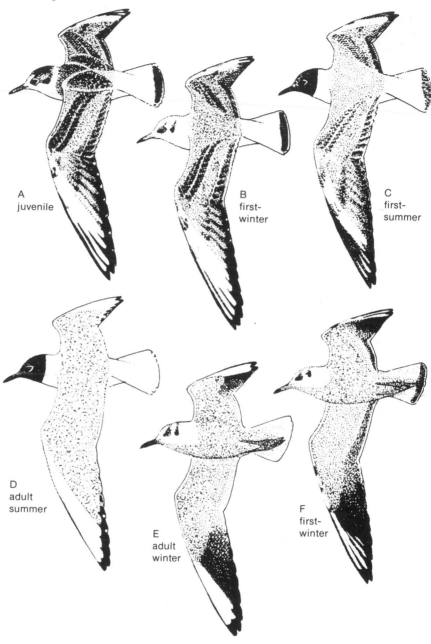

Fig. 5. **Black-headed Gulls** *Larus ridibundus* in flight.

First-summer (Fig. 5C, underwing and tail similar to first-winter, 5F. When standing similar to first-winter, 3A, but hood usually more extensive) Acquired by head and body moult, February to April. *As first-winter except:*

HEAD Dark chocolate-brown hood (fading to pale brown by mid-summer) of variable extent. (Field sample of 90 in May in southeast England showed 7% full hood; 58% white-flecked full hood; 24% more white than brown; 11% winter head pattern.)

BODY Hindneck and breast-sides off-white or grey-washed on individuals with winter head pattern.

WINGS AND TAIL Becoming extremely worn and faded on some by mid-summer.

BARE PARTS Legs and base of bill more orange, less flesh-coloured; prominent dark tip to bill.

Adult winter/second-winter (Fig. 5E, upperwing and tail patterns similar to adult summer, 5D) Acquired by complete moult late summer to October.

HEAD AND BODY Usually as first-winter, but exceptionally with extensive dark markings or even full summer hood in mid-winter. Exceptionally, underparts have pink flush of varying strength, rarely intense.

WINGS Primaries and primary coverts with more white than in first-year plumages, black restricted to outer web of 1st primary and primary tips inwards as far as 6th to 8th: pale grey tips to primaries usually from the 5th inwards. Remainder of wing pale grey, with thin white leading and trailing edges. From above and below, white leading edge to outer wing more extensive than in first-year plumages, and dark area on underside blacker and restricted to outer primaries, not extending onto secondaries. Underwing-coverts white or very pale grey.

TAIL All white.

BARE PARTS Bill red or bright red, with dark tip; legs red or bright red.

A few fail to acquire full adult plumage in their second winter, showing dark markings, especially on the greater primary coverts and alula, usually undetectable in the field. Obvious black lines or fringes on the outer webs of the 2nd and 3rd primaries are probably an indication of second-year plumage. Individuals with orange-yellow bill with dark tip, and orange-flesh legs, may be confidently aged as second-years which have yet to acquire the adult bare part colour. Variation in the number of primaries with black and the number and extent of the pale grey tips does not seem to be connected with age. Individuals with normal adult summer plumage except for white flecks in the brown hood and paler bare parts are probably in second-summer plumage.

Adult summer/second-summer (Fig. 5D, underwing and tail similar to adult winter, 5E) Acquired by head and body moult, January to April. *As adult winter except:*

HEAD Dark chocolate-brown hood (fading to pale brown by mid-summer) fully developed, darker around rear margin, with prominent white crescents posteriorly above and below eye, forming broken eye-ring.

BODY some show pink flush of variable strength on underparts, rarely intense.

WINGS Pale grey tips to inner primaries reduced or lacking.

BARE PARTS Iris brown. Orbital ring and bill wholly dark maroon-red, only slightly paler in tone than brown of head; mouth and gape bright red. Legs dark red.

Slender-billed Gull
Larus genei

(Figs. 3B and 7, Photographs 23–36)

Adult summer

IDENTIFICATION

The slightly longer wings, longer legs and heavier body than Black-headed Gull are noticeable only when the two species are together. In flight, the tail looks slightly longer and fuller, as if to counterbalance the elongated head and neck: the tail is not wedge-shaped, contrary to some statements in the literature, but the central one or two pairs of tail feathers on some individuals apparently protrude slightly further than the remainder. The peculiar shape of head, neck and bill is perhaps the most important field mark at all ages: Black-headeds can look long-necked at times, but they never have the almost grotesque, 'giraffe-necked' look of Slender-billed with its neck fully extended when alert or alarmed. The distance from the eye to the bill is greater than in the case of Black-headed, and the forehead is strikingly elongated, producing a peculiar 'snout' effect, which is further exaggerated by the longer bill: Black-headed rarely even suggests this appearance, having a more rounded head profile and shorter bill.

The first-year wing pattern differs from Black-headed by usually having a paler brown carpal-bar and less extensive black. The eye-crescent and ear-spot are much paler (both may be lacking on some), and the paler bill (with dark tip much smaller or completely lacking) and legs are further differences. Throughout the year the adult is instantly separable from Black-headed by the all-white head (occasionally with a faint grey ear-spot in winter), the pale eye (although breeding adults often look black-eyed, especially at long range), and by the usually strongly pink-flushed underparts (although this coloration may not be obvious at long range in bright sunlight).

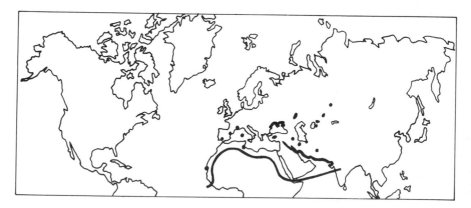

Fig. 6.   World distribution of **Slender-billed Gull** *Larus genei*, showing areas of proved breeding (solid black) and approximate southern limit of winter/non-breeding range (black line). Rare vagrant anywhere north of breeding range; up to 1981, three records in Britain and Ireland, all in coastal southeast England, in 1960, 1963 and 1971.

Grey-headed Gull has a head shape intermediate between Black-headed and Slender-billed, and, like the latter, has a long neck when alert, pale eyes when adult and pale head markings in winter; but its larger size, extensive black on the outer primaries at all ages, mainly dusky underwing without white and the darker grey tone of the wings are the most obvious differences.

AGEING SUMMARY

Juvenile: extensive grey-brown on head, mantle and scapulars (summer to late September).

First-winter: pale grey mantle and scapulars, pale brown carpal-bar, blackish secondary bar and tail band, pale grey ear-spot, pale bill and legs (July to April).

First-summer: faded, very pale brown carpal-bar, faded blackish secondary bar and tail band, pale bill and legs (March to October).

Adult winter/second-winter: adult wing and tail pattern, pale grey ear-spot usually present, faintly pink-flushed underparts, pale iris, dark bill and legs (August to March).

Adult summer/second-summer: adult wing and tail pattern, all-white head, pink-flushed underparts, pale iris, dark bill and legs (March to October).

DETAILED DESCRIPTIONS

Juvenile (Not illustrated, but wing and tail pattern similar to first-winter Figs 3B, 7A and 7C: head, body and bare parts as described below) *Basic pattern of plumage similar to juvenile Black-headed except:*
HEAD White, with pale buff and grey markings. Ear-spot and partial hood effect much less defined or lacking.
BODY Mantle, scapulars and sides of breast grey-brown, lacking rich ginger-brown coloration of Black-headed.
WINGS Carpal-bar paler brown, and blackish areas at tips of inner primaries less extensive, hence dark trailing edge to middle wing less prominent. White on outer primaries and primary coverts usually more extensive and black never so extensive as on some Black-headeds (cf. Fig. 5C).
BARE PARTS Iris dark brown perhaps quickly becoming pale (it is possible that some individuals never have a dark iris); orbital ring dark. Bill mainly pale orange-flesh, with dark tip small or lacking. Legs pale orange-flesh.

First winter (Figs. 3B, 7A and 7C) Acquired by post-juvenile head and body moult, which starts at fledging and is usually complete by late September. *Basic pattern of plumage similar to first-winter Black-headed except:*
HEAD White with dark eye-crescent and usually pale grey ear-spot.
BODY Underparts white, sometimes faintly tinged pink.
WINGS As juvenile, but brown and blackish areas faded paler.
BARE PARTS As juvenile, except most have pale iris at close range, and some may show reddish bill and orbital ring. (See summary at end of first-summer description.)

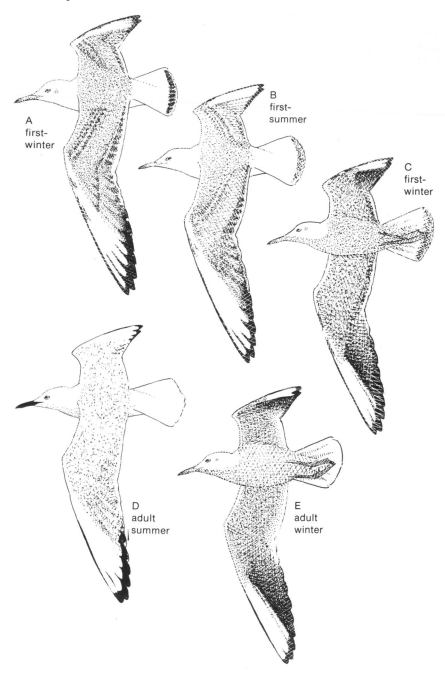

Fig. 7.   **Slender-billed Gulls** *Larus genei* in flight.

First-summer (Fig. 7B, underwing and tail similar to first-winter, 7C. When standing, similar to first-winter, 3B, but carpal-bar and ear-spot usually lacking.) Acquired by head and body moult, February to April. *Appearance as first-winter except:*

HEAD Pale grey ear-spot usually lacking.

WINGS AND TAIL Invariably becoming very worn and faded, so that pale brown carpal-bar (and sometimes even dark secondaries) appear hardly darker than grey of mantle and rest of wings.

BARE PARTS Iris pale; orbital ring usually reddish. Bill and legs orange-flesh or pale orange, and some may acquire hint of adult coloration by late summer.

Because of their general paleness, some distant perched first-year birds are separable from adults only by paler bill and legs, and (in summer) by lack of strongly pink-flushed underparts; in flight, first-year wing pattern and banded tail are obvious.

Adult winter/second-winter (Fig. 7E, wing and tail pattern similar to adult summer, 7D) Acquired by complete moult, late summer to October.

HEAD AND BODY As first-winter, except eye-crescent and ear-spot often lacking, and underparts pink-flushed to variable extent and strength.

WINGS AND TAIL As adult Black-headed, but white on outer primaries more extensive, giving more prominent white leading edge to outer wing.

BARE PARTS Iris white, pale yellow or greenish. Bill dark red or orange-red, looking black at distance. Legs not so dark as bill, with more orange tone.

Adult summer/second-summer (Fig. 7D, underwing and tail as adult winter, 7E) Acquired by head and body moult, February to April. *As adult winter, except:*

HEAD All white, sometimes with pale pink flush.

BODY Whole underparts with usually strong pink flush, strongest on breast and belly.

BARE PARTS Iris white, pale yellow, greenish or greenish-grey: breeding individuals often look black-eyed, especially at long range; orbital ring red. Bill dark blood-red with blackish tip, darker than adult summer Black-headed and looking black at distance. Legs slightly less dark than bill.

Bonaparte's Gull
Larus philadelphia

(Figs. 3c and 9, Photographs 37–47)

Adult summer

IDENTIFICATION

This attractive small gull is a miniature version of Black-headed, between Black-headed and Little Gull in size. Size and the combination of quicker wingbeat, whiter underwing, neat blackish bill and surface-picking feeding suggest a tern-like appearance, although this is more illusory than actual in terms of wing shape and flight action. The small size and the neatly black-bordered white (not extensively dusky as on Black-headed) underwing with translucent outer primaries are among the best distinctions from the others in this group at all ages. Some worn and faded first-summer Black-headeds can seem to have a translucent underwing at times, but this impression is usually fleeting.

In first-year plumages, there are several other differences from Black-headed. The smaller bill is black, sometimes with a reddish base (pale with dark tip in the case of Black-headed). The carpal-bar is darker brown and looks blackish at a distance. Unlike Black-headed, the inner primaries have neat white terminal spots (although these are subject to wear), and the subterminal black forms a thinner, neater black rear border to the middle wing. The outer greater primary coverts are mainly blackish, while the inner ones are plain grey, the reverse of the pattern on Black-headed Gull. The grey mantle and scapulars are a shade darker (obviously so in dull light), and, on first-winters, this colour extends onto the hindneck and breast-sides much more strongly than on Black-headed Gull.

Adults, as well as having the size and underwing differences, are further distin-

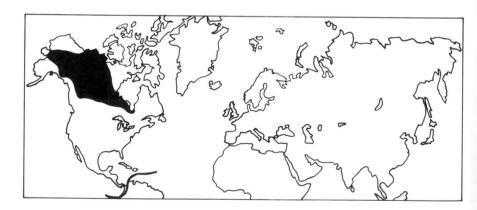

Fig. 8.   World distribution of **Bonaparte's Gull** *Larus philadelphia*, showing approximate breeding range (solid black) and approximate southern limit of winter/non-breeding range (black line). Vagrant to western coastal Europe, with average of one or two records annually in Britain and Ireland.

guished from Black-headed by all-black bill, blackish-grey hood in summer, with more prominent white crescents above and below the eye, usually strong pink flush on the underparts (rarely so on Black-headed), and (in winter) grey hindneck and breast-sides.

First-year Little Gull (p. 107) is smaller than Bonaparte's. The carpal-bar is blackish and the outer upperwing lacks the extensive white on the leading edge, although, when the wing is fully spread, the white inner webs of the outer primaries give a lined black-and-white appearance. The underwing is mainly white, lacking the translucent area on the outer primaries. Little Gull has a neat dark cap in winter and first-summer plumages, which Bonaparte's lacks.

AGEING SUMMARY

Juvenile: extensive blackish head markings and rich brown on mantle, scapulars, back and breast-sides (summer to late September).

First-winter: pale grey mantle and scapulars, dark brown carpal-bar, black secondary bar and tail band, winter head pattern (July to April).

First-summer· faded brown carpal-bar, blackish secondary bar and tail band, hood developed to variable extent (March to October).

Adult winter/second-winter: adult wing pattern, all-white tail, winter head pattern (August to March).

Adult summer/second-summer: adult wing pattern, all-white tail, fully developed hood (February to October).

DETAILED DESCRIPTIONS

Juvenile (Fig. 9A shows an individual in moult from juvenile to first-winter. Underwing and tail similar to first-winter, 9F). *Basic pattern of plumage similar to juvenile Black-headed except:*
HEAD Markings blacker with less brown. Ear-spot darker and more defined, and often with clear-cut cap.
BODY Mantle, scapulars, back and breast-sides brown, without ginger tone.
WINGS Carpal-bar darker brown, looking blackish at distance. From above, pattern of primaries and secondaries is similar, but primaries from 3rd inwards usually prominently tipped white, and less black on 4th inwards, giving thinner, neater, dark trailing edge. Figs. 9A (with most black) and 9B (with least black) show extent of normal variation. Inner web of all primaries white (except for black tip), and lacks complete broad dusky border, this difference visible on upperwing as cleaner grey inner primaries, and on underwing as neat, thin black border; area of translucent white in triangle along leading edge; and lack of dusky on inner primaries. Outer primary coverts mainly blackish, inner ones mainly grey.
BARE PARTS Iris dark brown. Bill black, or with small pale area at base. Mouth flesh. Legs pale flesh.

First-winter (Figs 3C, 9B and 9F) Acquired by post-juvenile head and body moult, which starts at fledging and is usually complete by late September. *Basic pattern of plumage similar to first-winter Black-headed except:*

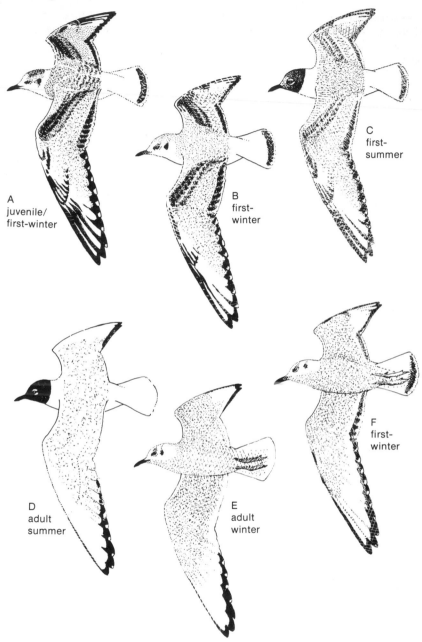

Fig. 9.   **Bonaparte's Gulls** *Larus philadelphia* in flight.

HEAD Ear-spot usually blacker and more defined. Hindneck (and sometimes nape and crown) obviously grey, (extension of mantle colour), not very pale grey or white as Black-headed.

BODY Mantle, scapulars and back uniform grey, darker than Black-headed, sometimes with a few retained brown juvenile feathers.

WINGS As juvenile, but white primary tips reduced.

BARE PARTS Much as juvenile, but bill often with some red at base.

First-summer (Fig. 9C, underwing and tail similar to first-winter, 9F. On the ground, similar to first-winter 3C, but hood usually more extensive) Acquired by head and body moult, February to April. *As first-winter, except:*

HEAD Black usually more extensive, and a few may acquire full hood and lose grey hindneck.

WINGS Becoming worn and faded by late summer, white primary tips may disappear.

TAIL Central feathers sometimes included in spring moult, thus white, breaking tail band. White tail fringes may disappear through wear.

BARE PARTS Much as juvenile.

Adult winter/second-winter (Fig. 9E, wing and tail pattern as adult summer, 9D) Acquired by complete moult, July to October.

HEAD AND BODY As first-winter but underparts may be slightly flushed pink.

WINGS Upperwing similar to adult Black-headed, but, from below, primaries lack extensive blackish: instead they are white with translucent triangle along leading edge, bordered along rear edge by thin black line formed by tips to outer six to nine primaries.

TAIL White.

BARE PARTS Iris dark brown. Bill black, sometimes with some red at base. Legs flesh to reddish-orange.

A few fail to acquire full adult plumage at this age, showing dark markings especially among greater primary coverts and rarely on tail: these faint marks probably rarely visible in field.

Adult summer/second-summer (Fig. 9D, underwing and tail as adult winter, 9E) Acquired by head and body moult, January to April. *As adult winter except:*

HEAD Full blackish-grey hood with prominent white crescents above and below eye, thickest at rear. Nape and hindneck white.

BODY Variable pink flush on underparts, usually obvious.

WINGS As adult winter, but whitish tips to primaries reduced or lacking.

BARE PARTS Orbital ring black. Bill black. Mouth orange-red. Legs orange-red.

Grey-headed Gull
Larus cirrocephalus

(Figs. 3D and 11, Photographs 48–59)

Adult summer

IDENTIFICATION

The Grey-headed Gull is unfamiliar to most European observers, yet the record of one in Spain (Ree 1973) shows that it may occur elsewhere in southern Europe or even Britain.

It is the largest member of this group, between Common Gull and Black-headed in size. Compared with Black-headed, it is broader-winged and, when gliding, the wings are held flatter and less angled, giving a 'sail-plane' appearance. On the ground, it has a more upright carriage, with longer legs, and, when alert, has a 'head up, tail down' posture. It is longer-necked than Black-headed, with a sloping forehead and heavier and longer bill, recalling Slender-billed Gull. These size and structural differences are among its best field marks at all ages.

In first-year plumages, other differences from Black-headed are the darker grey of the wings, mantle and scapulars, all-black outer primaries and less extensive white on the leading edge of the outer upperwing, wholly dusky underwing, thinner black tail band and usually less well-defined head markings.

Grey-headed is the only one in this group which regularly takes an extra year to reach adult plumage, as might be expected in view of its larger size: second-years are fairly readily distinguishable in the field, as described in the detailed descriptions of second-winter and second-summer.

To some European eyes, adults may recall Common Gull rather than Black-headed because of the larger size, broader wings, darker grey upperparts and the prominent

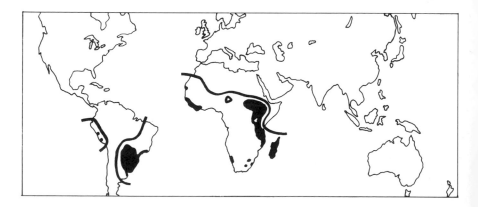

Fig. 10.   World distribution of **Grey-headed Gull** *Larus cirrocephalus*, showing approximate breeding range (solid black) and approximate limits of winter/non-breeding range (black line). One European record: adult at Las Marismas, Spain, 20th June to 15th August 1971 (Ree 1973).

mirrors on the outer two primaries. The combination of extensive white on the leading edge of the upperwing and prominent mirrors gives a pattern diagnostic among western Palearctic gulls: this and the wholly blackish underwing, pale iris, and (in summer at least) pale dove-grey, white-faced hood, as well as the size and structural differences, give a strikingly distinctive appearance. Black-headed Gulls pass through a white-faced phase in autumn as the head moult progresses, giving a head pattern similar to that of Grey-headed.

AGEING SUMMARY

Juvenile: extensive grey-brown on head, mantle, scapulars and breast-sides. (See comments under detailed description of first-winter about timing of moults.)

First-winter: brown carpal-bar, blackish secondary bar and tail band, head mainly white with grey markings and ear-spot.

First-summer: brown carpal-bar, blackish secondary bar and tail band, hood developed to variable extent.

Second-winter: as adult, except dusky markings on secondaries and tertials forming darker trailing edge to inner wing. More black than white on outer upperwing, and white primary tips and mirrors small or lacking. Iris darker than adult and bare parts dull flesh. Head pattern as first-winter, or pale, ill-defined hood.

Second-summer: as second-winter, but bare parts nearer or matching colour of summer adult. Hood often fully developed.

Adult winter/third-summer: adult wing pattern; head pattern as first-winter, or pale, ill-defined hood; obvious white iris; bare parts duller than adult summer.

Adult summer/third-summer: adult wing pattern, full hood, dark red bill, red legs.

DETAILED DESCRIPTIONS

Juvenile (Not illustrated, but wing and tail pattern similar to first-winter, Figs. 3D, 11A and 11C: head, body and bare parts as described below)
HEAD White, with extensive grey-brown clouding, darker ear-spot and eye-crescent, forming partial hood, separated from mantle by whitish collar on upper hindneck. Thin white crescents above and below eye.
BODY Underparts white, with grey-brown breast-sides extending from mantle. Mantle and scapulars brown, with pale feather fringes giving obvious scaled effect on scapulars. Rump pale grey.
WINGS Pattern similar to juvenile Black-headed, but grey areas on inner upperwing slightly darker: outer wing has less white, outer two or three primaries wholly black. White on outer webs at base of 3rd or 4th to 5th or 6th primaries form patch in middle of outer wing which extends onto outer greater primary coverts. Inner four or five primaries and their coverts mainly grey, with blackish areas at tips which join with blackish secondary bar to form dark trailing edge. All but outer two or three primaries have tiny white spots at tips, increasing in size inwards. Inner web of all primaries blackish, and underwing-coverts grey, so that, from below, underwing

appears wholly dusky (but not so dark as adult's), except for two or three translucent spots which correspond with white area on upperwing.

TAIL White with neat black subterminal band, usually thinner than Black-headed's and often not extending to outer feathers: when tail fully spread, black may appear as separate spots.

BARE PARTS Iris brown. Bill pale flesh or yellowish-flesh, with extensive dark tip. Legs dull flesh or yellowish-flesh.

First-winter (Figs. 3D, 11A and 11C) Acquired by post-juvenile head and body moult, which starts at fledging and is usually complete within about two months. Published breeding records from Africa refer to the period April to September, but breeding may take place outside this period. The timing of the post-juvenile and later moults is fixed by the fledging date, so temporal limits cannot be fixed for the moults of this or other equatorial breeding species which have a variable season.

HEAD White, with pattern of dusky markings similar to Black-headed Gull, but often paler and less defined. Lower hindneck pale grey.

BODY Underparts and rump white. Mantle and scapulars uniform grey, without white scapular-crescent, and darker than Black-headed, sometimes with a few brown feathers retained from juvenile plumage.

WINGS As juvenile, but brown and blackish areas faded, and white primary tips and secondary fringes reduced.

TAIL As juvenile, but band faded and whitish terminal fringe reduced or lacking.

BARE PARTS Much as juvenile.

First-summer (Fig. 11B, underwing and tail similar to first-winter 11C. When standing, similar to first-winter, 3D, but carpal-bar paler and hood usually more extensive) Acquired by head and body moult, which starts about six months after fledging. *As first-winter except:*

HEAD Grey usually more extensive, and some may acquire adult hood and lose pale grey on lower hindneck.

WINGS AND TAIL Dark areas become much faded, especially brown carpal-bar, and white primary tips and terminal fringes on secondaries and tail often disappear.

Second-winter (Fig. 11D) Acquired by a complete moult, which starts about 12 months after fledging. Some may reach adult plumage at this age, but probably the majority take an extra year. *As adult winter except:*

WINGS Black usually more extensive than white on outer primaries, and white primary tips usually small or lacking. Mirrors, if present at all, usually smaller than on adults, or confined to outer primary. Tertials and secondaries with dusky centres, forming darker trailing edge to inner wing. Sometimes a few brown feathers among greater primary, median and lesser coverts.

BARE PARTS Iris usually becoming pale, but lacking full adult colour and looking dark at distance. Bill and legs dull flesh.

Second-summer (Wing and tail patterns similar to second-winter, Fig. 11D) Acquired by head and body moult, which begins about 18 months after fledging. *As second-winter except:*

HEAD Full adult hood usually acquired.

BARE PARTS Much as adult summer, but iris may remain darker.

Fig. 11. **Grey-headed Gulls** *Larus cirrocephalus* in flight.

Adult winter/third-winter (Fig 11F, wings and tail as adult summer, 11E) Acquired by complete moult, which starts towards the end of breeding activity. Some, probably a minority, may acquire adult plumage in their second winter.

HEAD Hood as first-winter or adult summer in extent, but paler and less defined, sometimes with ill-defined ear-spot.

BODY Mantle and scapulars uniform grey, without prominent scapular- or tertial-crescents, a shade darker than Black-headed Gull.

WINGS Inner wing uniform grey, darker than Black-headed. White more extensive than black on outer primaries, with prominent pear-shaped white mirrors on outer two. White tips, usually prominent, on 3rd or 4th to 7th or 8th primaries. Inner webs of primaries (except mirrors) wholly blackish and underwing-coverts grey, whole underwing thus appearing dusky, apart from a few translucent spots showing through fully spread wing, corresponding to white on upperside.

TAIL White.

BARE PARTS Iris pale yellow or whitish. Orbital ring red. Bill duller than adult summer, with variable subterminal dark tip. Legs paler than bill, duller than adult summer.

Adult summer/third-summer (Fig. 11E, underwing and tail as adult winter, 11F) Acquired by head and body moult, which starts before the beginning of breeding activity. *As adult winter, except:*

HEAD Hood fully developed, extending farther down throat and nape than on Black-headed Gull, darkest posteriorly and shading from dove-grey to whitish on forehead and chin. Thin white crescents above and below eye. Hindneck white.

BODY Sometimes with faint pink flush on underparts.

WINGS Whitish tips on primaries reduced or lacking.

BARE PARTS Bill red, much darker than hood and looking black at distance. Legs red, brighter than bill.

Common, Mediterranean, Ring-billed, Laughing and Franklin's Gulls

The five species in this group share a similar first-year plumage pattern of blackish outer primaries and secondary bar, extensive brownish carpal-bar, more or less defined tail band, and mainly white or lightly marked underparts. Herring *Larus argentatus*, Lesser Black-backed *L. fuscus*, Great Black-backed *L. marinus*, Audouin's *L. audouinii* and Great Black-headed Gulls *L. ichthyaetus* (group 3) have some rather similar immature patterns, but at least their much greater size should be obvious and avoid confusion between the two groups, except perhaps in the case of Ring-billed Gull *L. delawarensis* and Herring Gull. Adult Mediterranean *L. melanocephalus*, Laughing *L. atricilla* and Franklin's Gulls *L. pipixcan* are hooded in summer, and Ring-billed Gull is the only one with pale eyes when adult.

All normally reach adult plumage in their third winter: second-years are normally readily aged, mainly by the pattern of the outer wing, and, in the cases of Ring-billed and Laughing Gulls, often also by traces of a dark secondary bar and tail band. Franklin's Gull has a complete moult in spring and another in autumn, unlike any other gull, and normally reaches adult plumage in its second summer, a shorter period of immaturity, which might be expected in view of its small size.

While the Common Gull *L. canus* is abundant in most of the western Palearctic (Fig. 13), the Mediterranean Gull is uncommon in much of the area (Fig. 15), and Ring-billed, Laughing and Franklin's Gulls are rare vagrants from America (Figs. 17, 19 & 21).

Table 2: Measurements (mm) of five gulls Larus *(from Dwight 1925)*

	sample	wing	tail	bill	tarsus
Common Gull *L. canus*	16	320–385	124–148	30–38	48–58
Mediterranean Gull *L. melanocephalus*	21	282–311	113–127	31–38	47–53
Ring-billed Gull *L. delawarensis*	23	335–392	134–162	36–46	52–62
Laughing Gull *L. atricilla*	26	295–330	113–133	35–44	46–55
Franklin's Gull *L. pipixcan*	26	262–286	97–111	27–34	39–45

Fig. 12.   First-winter **Ring-billed** *Larus delawarensis*, **Mediterranean** *L. melanocephalus*, **Common** *L. canus*, **Franklin's** *L. pipixcan* and **Laughing Gulls** *L. atricilla*, showing comparative sizes, shapes and stances.

Familiarity with the appearance of Common Gull at all ages will greatly aid the recognition of the others in this group, especially Mediterranean and Ring-billed Gulls which it particularly resembles in first-year plumages. In second-year and adult plumages, all five are much more distinctive, although the differences between Common and Ring-billed Gulls remain obvious only at close range.

Common Gull
Larus canus

(Figs. 12c and 14, Photographs 60–78)

Adult summer

IDENTIFICATION

This is one of the most familiar and abundant gulls in much of the western Palearctic. It resembles adult and some immature plumages of the much larger and generally more abundant Herring Gull: at a distance (when the otherwise obvious size and bare part colour differences may be difficult to judge) it is best told by its proportionately much smaller, neater bill, thinner-winged, unlaboured flight, and much larger mirrors when adult. At long range at all ages, it is best told from Black-headed Gull by its lack of white on the leading edge of the outer wing at all ages, its less pointed wings and lack of a hood or dark ear-spot; at close range, the larger size, darker grey upperparts and lack of reddish on the bill and legs are further differences.

On the ground it often has a characteristically elegant look, caused by the compound effect of small bill, rounded head with 'gentle' expression, rather long wings and somewhat dainty gait. The first-year flight pattern is not shared by any other *common* medium-sized gull. Second-years and adults are best identified by the medium size, rather dark blue-grey upperparts, prominent white tertial-crescent when perched, and yellowish or greyish bare part colour.

The others in this group are told from Common Gull by a combination of characters as described in the respective species accounts. It is always worth checking the obvious character of Common Gull—size, bill shape, head pattern and tone of grey on the upper parts—to eliminate the possible presence of one of the others: Ring-billed is slightly larger with thicker bill and paler grey upperparts, and perched second-years

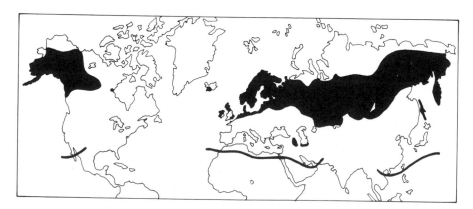

Fig. 13. World distribution of **Common Gull** *Larus canus*, showing approximate breeding range (solid black) and approximate southern limit of winter/non-breeding range (black line).

and adults lack the prominent white tertial-crescent. Mediterranean Gull is slightly smaller, usually with an obviously rather heavier bill; first-years have a clear-cut black streak behind the eye, much paler grey mantle and scapulars, more contrasting upperwing pattern, and whiter underwing. Second-year and adult Mediterranean and all ages of Laughing and Franklin's Gull have a distinctive appearance and are unlikely to be mistaken for Common Gulls.

AGEING SUMMARY

Juvenile: scaly brown mantle and scapulars, and extensive dusky markings on head and underparts (summer to September).

First-winter: dusky head and body markings, uniform grey mantle and scapulars, blackish outer primaries, secondary bar and tail band, brown carpal-bar, and black-tipped bill (July to April).

First-summer: as first-winter, but head and body whiter and wing pattern faded paler and contrasting with blue-grey mantle and scapulars (March to October).

Second-winter: wings uniform grey, with black tip not confined to primaries, but extending along leading edge of the outer wing, small mirrors, white primary tips tiny or lacking, and much dusky head streaking (July to April).

Second-summer: as second-winter, but head white or lightly marked (March to October).

Adult winter/third-winter: black of wing tip confined to primaries, large mirrors, prominent white primary tips (obvious when perched), dusky head markings, and bill pale, usually with thin dark subterminal mark or band. (August to March).

Adult summer/third summer: as adult winter, but head white and bill yellowish-green (March to October).

DETAILED DESCRIPTIONS

Juvenile (Fig. 14A. Underwing and tail similar to first-winter, 14D)

HEAD Forehead white, throat and nape whitish. Ear-coverts and crown densely streaked grey-brown, sometimes forming ill-defined partial hood. Thin white crescents above and below eye and dusky eye-crescent.

BODY Lower hindneck, flanks and often defined broad breast band uniform, mottled or streaked grey-brown. Belly and vent white. Mantle and scapulars buff, with neat pale feather fringes most prominent on scapulars. Rump and upper- and undertail-coverts white, with dark arrowhead markings or bars.

WINGS Carpal-bar brown, with rounded brown centres and pale fringes, and tertials with rather broad ill-defined whitish fringes. Greater coverts (except three or four innermost) uniform pale grey-brown, forming pale midwing panel. Outer greater primary coverts and outer three to five primaries wholly blackish-brown: dull grey on outer webs and terminal whitish fringes increasing in extent (and subterminal blackish areas decreasing) from 5th or 6th inwards, forming pale division between outer primaries and secondary bar. Underwing whitish, axillaries and most coverts with dark fringes, forming lines.

TAIL White, with clear-cut, broad, blackish-brown subterminal band.

BARE PARTS Iris dark brown. Bill blackish with pale base. Legs and base of bill flesh-pink or greyish.

First-winter (Figs. 12c, 14B and 14D) Acquired by post-juvenile head and body moult, which starts at fledging and is usually complete by late September.

HEAD As juvenile, but whiter.

BODY Lower hindneck, breast or breast-sides and flanks with variable grey-brown mottling, streaks or spots, most dense on lower hindneck and breast-sides; underparts otherwise white. Mantle and scapulars uniform blue-grey. Dark marks on rump and upper- and undertail coverts less prominent than juvenile or lacking.

WINGS AND TAIL As juvenile, but brown and blackish areas faded paler.

BARE PARTS As juvenile, but bill with clear-cut black tip. Legs and base of bill usually greyish.

First-summer (Fig. 14c. Underwing and tail similar to first-winter, 14D) Acquired by head and body moult, February to April. *As first-winter except:*

HEAD AND BODY Often whiter, less streaked: often wholly white.

WINGS AND TAIL Brown and grey areas becoming very faded, often almost uniform whitish, and black areas browner, often bleached light brown, especially primary tips. Wings, therefore, pale and contrasting with fresh blue-grey mantle and scapulars, giving saddle effect.

BARE PARTS Base of bill typically yellowish-flesh, but also greenish or greyish. Legs blue-grey or greyish-flesh.

Second-winter (Fig. 14E) Acquired by complete moult, June to October.

HEAD AND BODY As first-winter, but dark markings usually less extensive, especially on breast-sides and flanks. Rump and upper- and undertail coverts white.

WINGS AND TAIL As adult, but black extending to 6th to 8th primary and along leading edge of forewing onto greater and median primary coverts and alula; primaries lack prominent white tips, and mirrors on outer two are smaller. Some have a few brown-centred median and lesser coverts and small blackish marks centrally on the tertials; individuals showing prominent traces of secondary bar or tail band are rare.

BARE PARTS Iris brown. Bill typically blue-grey or grey-green, occasionally yellowish, with dark tip or subterminal band. Legs blue-grey or greyish flesh.

Second-summer (wing and tail pattern similar to second-winter, Fig. 14E) Acquired by head and body moult, February to April. *As second-winter except:*

HEAD AND BODY Usually white or lightly marked.

WINGS Black areas faded browner, and tiny white primary tips reduced or lacking.

Adult winter/third-winter (wing and tail pattern as adult summer, Fig. 14F) Acquired by complete moult, late summer to October.

HEAD White, with fine dark streaks and spots most dense on lower hindneck. Eye-crescent dusky, and thin white crescents above and below eye.

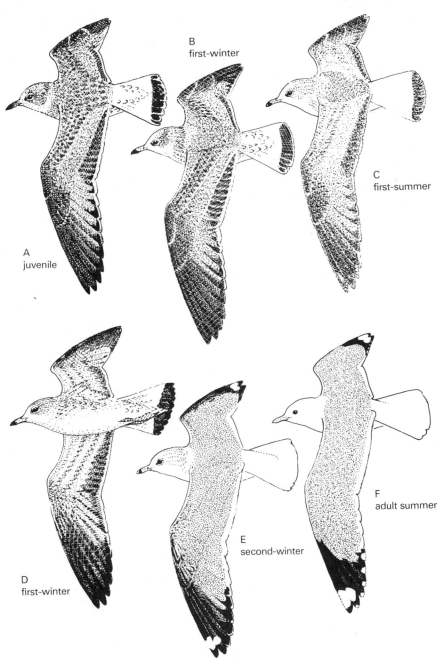

Fig. 14. **Common Gulls** *Larus canus* in flight.

BODY Underparts and rump white, sometimes a few dark spots and streaks on breast-sides and flanks. Mantle, scapulars and back uniform blue-grey with small white scapular-crescents.

WINGS Clear-cut black above and below on wing-tip confined to primaries and extending inwards to 5th or 6th; prominent white tips to all except 1st, and large mirrors on outer two (larger on 1st than 2nd). Remainder of wing uniform blue-grey, with thin white leading edge (marginal coverts) and scapular crescent and broad white trailing edge and tertial-crescent. Underwing-coverts white.

TAIL White.

BARE PARTS Iris brown. Bill yellowish, often with greyish base and usually a faint dark subterminal mark or band. Legs yellowish, greenish, or greyish, often tinged flesh.

Adult summer/third-summer (Fig. 14F) Acquired by head and body moult, February to April. *As adult winter except:*

HEAD White.

BODY Underparts white.

WINGS White primary tips reduced or lacking.

BARE PARTS Orbital ring red. Bill usually wholly yellow or yellowish-green. Mouth flesh; gape orange.

Mediterranean Gull
Larus melanocephalus

(Figs. 12B and 16, Photographs 79–93)

Second-summer

IDENTIFICATION

Past comparison between Mediterranean and Black-headed Gulls is somewhat misleading. When perched, there is a rather superficial resemblance at all ages, but the distinctive appearance of Mediterranean Gull in second-year and adult plumages render it unlikely to be overlooked. In first-year plumages, especially in flight, it is much more likely to be dismissed as a Common Gull, owing to its similar flight pattern. It is, however, smaller than Common Gull (nearer to Black-headed) with a marginally stouter bill which (mainly due to its dark colour) often appears blob-ended or heavy and drooping. It appears longer-legged and has a strutting gait, often with head hunched between the shoulders. In flight it appears heavy-bodied and bull-necked, with less angled wings, stiffer wingbeats and less spread tail.

First-years differ further from Common Gull in having blacker outer primaries and secondary bar, and paler grey midwing panel, giving a more contrasting upperwing pattern. The extensive white on the inner webs of the outermost primaries is sometimes visible from above when the wing is fully spread (Common Gull has all-dark outer primaries), and the underwing is much whiter, with the dark outer primaries and secondary bar showing prominently through the wing. The tail band is thinner, especially at the sides. The underparts and head are white, the latter with dark markings of variable extent, in winter usually confined to more or less

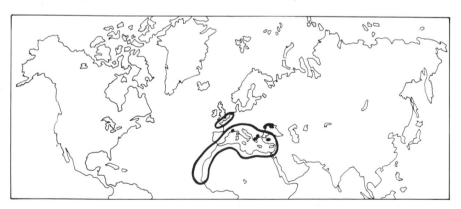

Fig. 15. World distribution of **Mediterranean Gull** *Larus melanocephalus*, showing approximate breeding range (solid black) and approximate limits of winter/non-breeding range (black line). Has bred Hungary, German Democratic Republic, Austria, Estonian SSR, Netherlands, Belgium, France and England. Increasing in recent years in Britain, with over 100 records annually, mainly in southern coastal areas, where present spasmodic breeding of a few pairs is likely to lead to permanent colonisation in the near future.

well-defined fine dark streaking behind the eye. In first-winter and subsequent plumages, the grey of the upperparts is pale pearly-grey, much paler than on Common Gull. Juveniles have a neat scaly pattern on the scapulars and a surprisingly plain head (usually with no more than a hint of the first-winter pattern) and white underparts with a faintly mottled, pale grey breast band and flanks: the rather plain head and underparts, lacking any obvious dark streaking, and the neat scaly upperparts, give juveniles a smart, clean appearance. Bill and leg colour is highly variable in the first year, darker than Common Gull or with striking orange or reddish coloration.

Second-years and adults have a distinctive appearance, which is unlikely to be confused with any other species of gull. Second-years are readily aged by the black markings near the tips of the outer primaries. Adults have a black outer web on the outermost primary (rarely two outermost), but otherwise the wings and upperparts are pale pearly-grey, shading to white on the secondary and primary tips. In summer, the hood is black and extends farther down the nape than on Black-headed Gull, and the bill is scarlet, strikingly paler in tone than the black hood (Black-headed Gull lacks this bill/hood contrast), often with a dark subterminal mark and yellowish tip; the legs are scarlet.

AGEING SUMMARY

Juvenile: scaly grey-brown mantle and scapulars (summer to September).

First-winter: uniform pale grey mantle and scapulars, blackish outer primaries, secondary bar and tail band, brown carpal-bar, winter head pattern (July to April).

First-summer: as first-winter, but hood sometimes developed to variable extent, wing pattern faded, and brown carpal-bar reduced or lacking (March to October).

Second-winter: as adult winter, except for variable amount of black near tips of outer primaries (July to April).

Second-summer: as second-winter, but hood often fully developed (March to October).

Adult winter/third-winter: adult wing pattern (black confined to outer web of outer primary), winter head pattern (August to March).

Adult summer/third-summer: adult wing pattern, full black hood (February to October).

DETAILED DESCRIPTIONS

Juvenile (Fig. 16A. Underwing and tail similar to first-winter, 16D)
HEAD White, creamy or buff-washed. Rear ear-coverts and extension over rear crown greyish, giving faint trace of first-winter head-pattern. Eye-crescent blackish; thin white crescents above and below eye.
BODY Underparts and rump white, except for broad band across breast extending onto flanks pale grey-buff with darker mottling. Lower hindneck and mantle grey with fine pale feather fringes giving frosty appearance; scapulars grey-brown with

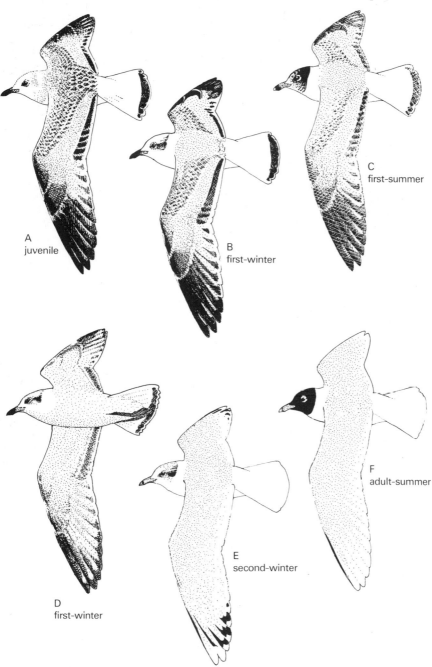

Fig. 16. **Mediterranean Gulls** *Larus melanocephalus* in flight.

darker subterminal crescent and neat pale buff or whitish fringes giving strong scaly pattern.

WINGS Carpal-bar dark grey-brown or brown with paler feather fringes; median coverts with darker shaft-streaks and subterminal crescents. Tertials dark-centered with clear-cut whitish fringes. Inner three or four greater coverts dark-centred, remainder clear pale grey, forming pale midwing panel. Secondaries black, with fine white edges and broad tips. Outer webs of outer five or six primaries and their coverts mainly black; inner primaries mainly grey, with subterminal black marks decreasing in size inwards; inner webs of primaries have extensive white, reaching nearly to tips; sometimes, outer primary (rarely outer two) all-black. Greater primary coverts tipped paler. Underwing mainly white, with many fewer dark markings on coverts than Common Gull.

TAIL White with clear-cut black subterminal band, narrower and often broken on outer feathers.

BARE PARTS Iris dark brown. Bill mainly blackish, with a usually small area of pale grey or flesh at base. Legs blackish.

First-winter (Figs. 12B, 16B and 16D) Acquired by post-juvenile head and body moult, which starts at fledging and is usually complete by late September. *As juvenile except:*

HEAD White with blackish markings of variable extent, typically rather clear-cut streak (or patch of fine streaks) from behind eye, often extending diffusely over rear crown, never an isolated round ear-spot as on Black-headed Gull.

BODY Underparts white. Mantle, scapulars and back uniform pale pearly-grey, same shade as grey of wings.

WINGS AND TAIL Brown of carpal-bar faded (often very ginger-brown), black areas slightly faded, and white tips and fringes of inner primaries, secondaries, tertials and tail reduced.

BARE PARTS Bill sometimes wholly blackish or brownish-black, but usually with pale base of variable extent, with clear-cut or diffuse blackish tip. Colour of base highly variable, from buff, flesh or yellowish, through orange to red. Legs similarly variable from blackish or grey (sometimes with olive-green tinge) through orange to red.

First-summer (Fig. 16C. Underwing and tail similar to first-winter, 16D) Acquired by head and body moult, February to April. *As first-winter except:*

HEAD Black head markings usually more extensive; a few acquire full hood.

WINGS AND TAIL Becoming very worn and faded in some, although black areas fade less than on most Common Gulls. A few replace most inner wing-coverts, and thus lack brown carpal-bar.

BARE PARTS Bill and leg colour highly variable, much as first-winter, but some may acquire near-adult coloration and bill pattern.

The least advanced individuals have dull bare parts, and wing and head patterns little different from first-winter, while the most advanced have adult-like bill and legs, well-developed or complete hood, and lack a carpal-bar.

Second-winter (Fig. 16E) Acquired by complete moult, May to September. *As adult winter except:*

WINGS Outer three to six primaries with subterminal black marks of variable extent and pattern. Outer greater primary coverts and alula occasionally with black marks.

BARE PARTS Bill flesh to reddish, with dark tip or subterminal band. Legs as adult winter or more orange-red.

It seems likely that a few advanced individuals may be indistinguishable from adult at this age.

Second-summer (Wing and tail pattern similar to second-winter, Fig. 16E) Acquired by head and body moult, February to April. *As second-winter except:*

HEAD Hood fully developed or with white flecking.

WINGS White primary tips reduced or lacking.

BARE PARTS Bill and legs much as adult summer.

Adult winter/third-winter (Wing and tail pattern as adult summer, Fig. 16F) Acquired by complete moult late summer to October.

HEAD AND BODY As first-winter.

WINGS Pale pearly-grey; primaries shading to white at tips; 1st (and rarely 2nd) with thin black line of variable extent on outer web. Secondaries and underwing white.

TAIL White.

BARE PARTS Bill pink, orange, red or blackish with dark tip or subterminal smudge or band, and often yellowish at extreme tip; legs orange, red or blackish.

Adult summer/third-summer (Fig. 16F) Acquired by head and body moult, January to April. *As adult winter except:*

HEAD Hood jet black, extending farther down nape than on Black-headed Gull. Prominent white crescent posteriorly above and below eye.

BARE PARTS Iris brown. Orbital ring scarlet. Bill scarlet, with or without thin blackish subterminal smudge or band, often with yellow or orange at extreme tip. Mouth scarlet. Legs scarlet.

Ring-billed Gull
Larus delawarensis

(Figs. 12A and 18, Photographs 94–111)

First-winter

IDENTIFICATION

Ring-billed Gull resembles Common Gull but (compared with the European race *L. c. canus*) usually is obviously slightly larger and heavier-bodied, with thicker bill, slightly longer legs, and more fierce expression caused by its less rounded head, often faint dark furrow or brow over the eye, and (on second-summer and older) pale iris. The grey of the upperparts is much paler, and perched second-years and older lack prominent white scapular- and tertial-crescents which are obvious on Common Gull. It has a plover-like gait, perhaps an effect of its slightly longer legs.

The heavier structure, fierce expression, and pale grey upperparts may recall Herring Gull (p. 78), and a small or small-looking individual of that species is probably the major identification pitfall, especially one in second-year plumage, the general plumage pattern and bare parts coloration of which could resemble that of a first-year Ring-billed.

In first-year plumages, further differences from Common Gull are the more contrasting upper- and underwing patterns (due mainly to the darker brown carpal-bar and the blacker outer primaries and secondary bar), the usually more variegated pattern of the tail band, the usually clearly spotted (rather than mottled) lower hindneck, and the usually more defined spots or crescentic markings on the breast-sides and flanks (rather than the usually indistinct mottling on Common Gull), although these may be reduced or lacking in first-summer plumage. The brown centres of the tertials tend to be darker, with thinner whitish fringes, and the dark

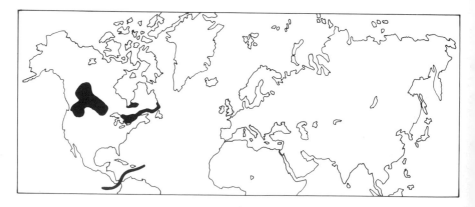

Fig. 17.   World distribution of **Ring-billed Gull** *Larus delawarensis*, showing approximate breeding range (solid black) and approximate southern limit of winter/non-breeding range (black line). Vagrant to Europe; in Britain and Ireland, small numbers now recorded annually since first record in 1973, and unprecedented influx of over 50 in 1981.

centres of the inner median and lesser coverts (which form the inner part of the carpal-bar) have a pointed shape at the tip, not rounded as on Common Gull, but these differences are valid only in fresh plumage because wear and fading eventually make the wing coverts uniform and whitish in both species. The inner greater coverts are often not plain grey-brown as on Common Gull, but are marked or barred with dark. The underwing and upper- and undertail coverts are on average more strongly barred than on Common Gull. Because of the paleness of the grey upperparts, Ring-billed lacks the contrasting dark grey saddle which is obvious on first-year (especially first-summer) Common Gulls. The band on the bill, and the clear yellow colour of the bill and legs, begin to develop during the first summer; Common Gull invariably retains a dark-tipped bill and greyish legs throughout the first year.

Second-years resemble adults, but are readily aged by the more extensive black on the leading edge of the outer wing, extending strongly onto the greater primary coverts and alula; unlike Common Gull, they have only one small mirror, if any, and most have prominent traces of a tail band and sometimes also a partial secondary bar which are rarely shown by second-year Common Gulls. The yellow on the bill and legs, and the thick, clear-cut black band on the bill are usually well developed by the second year; Common Gulls may also have a band on the bill in second-year and adult winter plumages, but it is usually less well-defined and quickly becomes thinner than on Ring-billed Gull, and the legs often remain greyish throughout the second year. Adult and some second-year Ring-billeds have a pale iris; the others in this group are dark-eyed at all ages. The wing-tip pattern of adults is close to that of Herring Gull, with mirrors much smaller than on Common Gull.

AGEING SUMMARY

Juvenile: scaly brown mantle and scapulars, and extensive dark markings on head, breast and flanks (summer to September).

First-winter: dusky head and body markings, grey mantle and scapulars, blackish outer primaries, secondary bar and tail band, brown carpal-bar, and black-tipped bill (July to April).

First-summer: as first-winter, but head and body whiter, wing pattern faded paler, and band on bill usually beginning to develop (March to September).

Second-winter: wings uniform grey, with black tip extending along leading edge of outer wing, one small mirror (or none), white primary tips tiny or lacking, usually traces of tail band and sometimes secondary bar, and much dusky on head (June to April).

Second-summer: as second-winter, but head white or lightly marked. Yellow bill colour and band usually well developed (March to October).

Adult winter/third-winter: black on wing-tip confined to primaries, usually two mirrors, prominent white primary tips (obvious when perched), dusky head markings, clear-cut black band on yellowish bill, and yellowish legs (August to March).

Adult summer/third-summer: as adult winter, but head white, white primary tips may be reduced or lacking, clear-cut black band on bill, and bill and legs bright yellow (March to October).

DETAILED DESCRIPTIONS

Juvenile (not illustrated, but wing and tail pattern similar to first-winter, Figs. 12A and 18A) *Resembles juvenile Common Gull except:*

BODY Lower hindneck, breast (especially breast-sides) and flanks more coarsely marked with darker grey-brown, usually with coarser pattern of distinct chevrons, crescentic markings or complex barring especially on breast-sides and flanks. Mantle and scapulars grey-brown, individual feathers with dark subterminal crescents and pale fringes forming more complex pattern than on Common Gull.

WINGS Dark areas on outer wing generally blacker, and more defined and less extensive on inner primaries: inner primaries and midwing panel basically paler grey, giving more contrasting upperwing pattern than on Common Gull. Inner greater coverts often with dark markings or bars, less uniformly grey-brown than on Common Gull. Carpal-bar darker, less brown, and tip of dark central area of individual median and lesser coverts (especially innermost) pointed, not rounded as on Common Gull. Tertials and adjacent greater coverts darker than Common Gull, with thinner pale fringes on average. Underwing coverts with darker markings on average, but some individuals have only faint barring.

TAIL Subterminal band rarely solid black and clear-cut as on Common Gull, but invariably broken by pale mottling of highly variable pattern: remainder of tail often shaded with grey of variable pattern. Tail pattern of Ring-billed Gulls highly variable, probably with any two individuals rarely identical, unlike comparatively standard pattern of Common Gull. Upper- and undertail coverts more strongly barred on average.

BARE PARTS Extreme tip of bill often whitish. Legs and base of bill typically flesh-pink.

First-winter (Figs. 12A and 18A. Underwing and tail similar to first-summer, 18E) Acquired by post-juvenile head and body moult which starts at fledging and is usually complete by late September. *As juvenile except:*

HEAD AND BODY Head and underparts usually generally whiter, with distinct blackish spots on lower hindneck, and defined spots and crescentic markings on breast-sides and flanks. Mantle and scapulars pale grey, some individual feathers often with dark subterminal crescents and fine pale fringes: mantle and scapulars thus paler grey, often with obvious faint barring or mottling, not uniform dark grey as on Common Gull. A few brown juvenile scapulars are sometimes retained.

WINGS AND TAIL Brown and blackish areas becoming faded, and white tips and fringes often reduced by wear.

First-summer (Figs. 18B and 18E) Acquired by head and body moult, February to April. *As first-winter except:*

HEAD AND BODY Dark markings reduced or completely lacking. Mantle and scapulars uniform pale grey.

WINGS AND TAIL Brown and grey areas often faded to whitish, and black areas faded browner, but contrast with pale grey saddle much less marked than on Common Gull. White tips and fringes reduced or lacking.

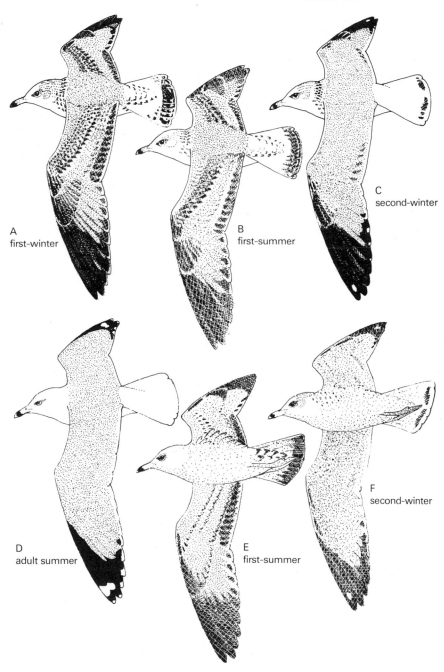

Fig. 18. **Ring-billed Gulls** *Larus delawarensis* in flight.

BARE PARTS Band on bill and yellowish coloration of bill and legs usually beginning to develop.

Second-winter (Figs. 18C and 18F) Acquired by complete moult, May to September. *Similar to second-winter Common Gull except:*

HEAD AND BODY Dark markings on hindneck and (if present at all) on breast-sides and flanks, more distinctly spotted. Mantle, scapulars and inner wing pale grey, much paler than Common Gull.

WINGS AND TAIL Only one mirror, if any, on 1st primary, often visible only from below. Most have prominent dark marks of highly variable (and often asymmetrical) pattern on tail, forming partial or broken tail band. Some also have dark marks on secondaries and tertials, forming partial secondary bar. White tertial fringes thin and shaded into pale grey remainder, thus lacking prominent tertial-crescent which is obvious on perched Common Gull. Underwing coverts sometimes faintly marked with dark.

BARE PARTS Pale iris. Thick black band on bill, and yellow of bill and legs well developed on most individuals.

Second-summer (wing and tail pattern similar to second-winter, Figs. 18C and 18F) Acquired by head and body moult, February to April. *As second winter except:*

HEAD AND BODY White, or with a few light spots on hindneck.

WINGS Black areas faded paler, and tiny white primary tips usually lacking through wear.

BARE PARTS Pale iris, thick band on bill and yellow of bill and legs well developed.

Adult winter/third-winter (wing and tail pattern as adult summer, Fig. 18D) Acquired by complete moult late summer to October. *Similar to adult winter Common Gull except:*

HEAD Dark markings more distinctly spotted.

BODY Mantle and scapulars (and inner wing) much paler grey.

WINGS White mirrors on 1st and 2nd primaries invariably much smaller, and tertial-crescent and white trailing edge to inner wing thinner and less defined.

BARE PARTS Pale yellowish iris, obvious at close range. Orbital ring dark. Bill with broad, clear-cut black subterminal band, dull yellow or yellow base and yellow tip. Legs yellowish.

Adult summer/third-summer (Fig. 18D) Acquired by head and body moult, February to April. *As adult winter except:*

HEAD White.

WINGS White primary tips reduced or lacking.

BARE PARTS Orbital ring and gape orange-red. Mouth orange-flesh. Legs and black-banded bill usually bright or deep yellow.

Laughing Gull
Larus atricilla

(Figs. 12E and 20, Photographs 112–130)

First-winter

IDENTIFICATION

Laughing Gull has a distinctive appearance at all ages, and is unlikely to be confused with any other gull except Franklin's.

Laughing is on average only slightly larger in body-size than Black-headed Gull, but because of its proportionately longer wings appears closer to Common Gull, especially in flight. It is smaller than Common Gull, but with proportionately longer wings (which give an attenuated look when perched and a rakish, long-winged silhouette in flight), longer bill (which often looks heavy and drooping) and longer legs. The grey of the upperparts is much darker than on Common Gull, close in tone to that of the British race of Lesser Black-backed Gull *L. f. graellsii.*

In first-winter plumage, the head, hindneck, breast, and flanks are extensively dark grey, shading to whitish on the chin, throat (often extending below and behind the dark ear-coverts to form a distinctive half-collar), forehead and belly. The coverts of the inner wing are mainly brown, contrasting with the mainly black outer wing and secondary bar. The underwing coverts are pale with dark tips, with a usually prominent diagonal dark bar extending from the axillaries. The tail is grey, with a broad black subterminal band, and the rump is white. First-summer plumage is similar, but often with a partial or full hood, and the wing-coverts are often faded to patchy pale brown.

Second-years closely resemble adults, but are readily aged by the more extensive black on the wing (extending strongly on to the greater primary coverts and alula), and most have traces of a secondary bar or tail band.

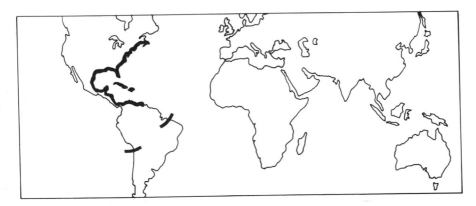

Fig. 19. World distribution of **Laughing Gull** *Larus atricilla*, showing approximate breeding range (solid black) and approximate southern limits of winter/non-breeding range (black line). Rare vagrant to Europe; in Britain and Ireland averaging two or three records annually.

Adults have uniform dark grey upperparts and wings, the latter with a broad white trailing edge, and black tip (*without* mirrors) confined to the outer primaries. In summer, the bill and legs are dull red, and the extensive black hood has prominent white crescents above and below the eye. In winter, the bill and legs are blackish, and the head has a dusky grey-and-black partial hood of variable extent, usually confined to behind the eye.

AGEING SUMMARY

Juvenile: scaly brown mantle and scapulars (summer to September).

First-winter: uniform grey mantle and scapulars, extensive grey on hindneck, breast and flanks, brown inner wing-coverts, blackish outer primaries and secondary bar, and white rump contrasting with grey tail, which has broad black subterminal band (July to April).

First-summer: as first winter, but less grey on hindneck and head, coverts of inner wing faded pale brown, and contrasting dark grey mantle and scapulars (March to October).

Second-winter: wings uniform grey, with black tip extending along leading edge of outer wing; white tips on primaries small or lacking; usually traces of secondary bar and tail band; winter head pattern; grey-washed breast-sides and flanks; and blackish bill and legs (July to April).

Second-summer: as second-winter, but hood partially or fully developed, underparts white and bill and legs usually dull reddish (March to October).

Adult winter/third-winter: black of wing tip mainly confined to primaries, which have obvious white tips; winter head pattern; bill blackish, with red line near tip of culmen; and legs blackish (August to March).

Adult summer/third-summer: as adult winter, but full black hood, white primary tips reduced or lacking, and dull red bill and legs (February to October).

DETAILED DESCRIPTIONS

Juvenile (not illustrated, but wing and tail pattern similar to first-winter, Figs 12E, 20A and 20C)

HEAD Mainly grey-brown, paler on forehead, lores, chin and throat, and often darker on rear ear-coverts, rear crown, and nape. Eye-crescent blackish, and thin whitish crescents above and below eye, less prominent than on subsequent plumages.

BODY Hindneck, broad breast-band, and flanks uniform grey-brown. Belly, vent and rump dull white. Mantle and scapulars brown, with pale buff feather fringes giving scaly appearance, most prominent on scapulars. Back uniform greyish.

WINGS Lesser and median coverts and tertials mainly brown like scapulars, with fine pale buff fringes; greater coverts grey-brown with whitish fringes. Secondaries black with fine white edges and broad white tips. Outer primaries and coverts wholly

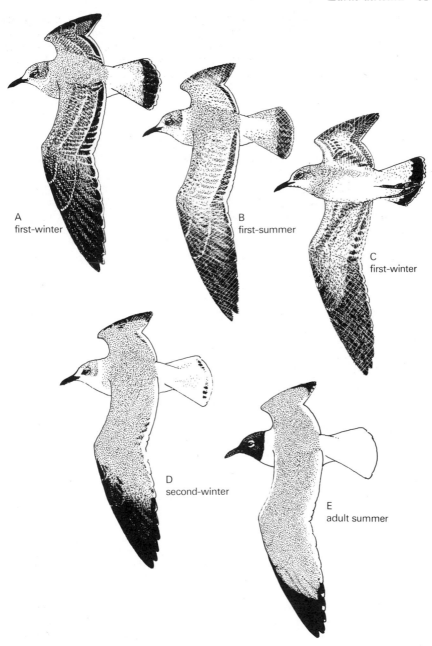

A
first-winter

B
first-summer

C
first-winter

D
second-winter

E
adult summer

Fig. 20. **Laughing Gulls** *Larus atricilla* in flight.

blackish, with thin white fringes at tips from 3rd to 5th inwards, and dull grey on outer and inner webs increasing from 4th to 6th inwards. Underwing coverts mainly dull white, with dusky markings and usually prominent diagonal dark bar extending from axillaries across median and lesser underwing coverts.

TAIL Outer webs dull grey, inner webs whitish, with broad black subterminal band always extending to the outer pair of feathers; thin white terminal fringe.

BARE PARTS Iris dark. Bill black, often with some dull brown at base. Legs blackish or dull brown.

First-winter (Figs 12E, 20A and 20C) Acquired by post-juvenile moult of head, body and variable number of coverts on inner wing, which starts at fledging and is usually complete by October. *As juvenile except:*

HEAD Mainly grey, with whitish forehead, lores, chin and throat, and darker patch on rear ear-coverts which often extends over rear crown and over crown above eye. White on throat often extends below and behind ear-coverts to form half-collar. White crescents above and below eye more prominent.

BODY Hindneck, breast-band, flanks, mantle and scapulars uniform dark grey.

WINGS Variable amount of new coverts on inner wing, especially median coverts, plain grey.

First-summer (Fig. 20B. Underwing and tail similar to first-winter, 20A) Acquired by head and body moult, February to April. *As first-winter except:*

HEAD Grey sometimes less extensive or with hood of variable extent.

BODY Grey on hindneck, breast and flanks may be less extensive.

WINGS AND TAIL Brown coverts of inner wing often much faded to patchy pale brown, and white terminal fringes to primaries, secondaries and tail reduced or lacking.

BARE PARTS Bill occasionally with reddish at tip of culmen.

Second-winter (Fig. 20D) Acquired by complete moult, June to late September.

HEAD White, with greyish patch of variable extent and strength on ear-coverts, usually extending over rear crown. Eye-crescent blackish. Crescents above and below eye white.

BODY Underparts and neck white, except for obvious pale grey wash on hindneck, breast-sides and flanks. Mantle and scapulars uniform dark grey, with prominent white tertial- and small white scapular-crescent when perched. Rump white.

WINGS Uniform dark grey, with prominent white trailing edge on secondaries and inner primaries. Small white tips on primaries from about 4th inwards. Usually, variable number of secondaries with blackish on outer webs, forming indistinct secondary bar. Outer four or five primaries black, extending along leading edge of outer wing onto coverts and alula. Subterminal black from 5th to 6th or 8th. Underwing-coverts white or grey-washed.

TAIL White, or with grey at base, often with black or grey subterminal spots of varying extent and pattern forming partial or broken tail band. Outer and central feathers white.

BARE PARTS As juvenile.

Second-summer (wing and tail pattern similar to second-winter, Fig. 20D) Acquired by head and body moult, February to April. *As second-winter except:*

HEAD Black usually more extensive, and most acquire full hood as adult summer.
BODY Grey clouding on breast-sides and flanks usually lacking.
BARE PARTS Bill usually dull red, or with blackish near tip, or red tip. Legs dull red or blackish-brown.

Adult winter/third-winter (wing and tail pattern as adult summer, Fig. 20E) Acquired by complete moult, late summer to October. *As second-winter except:*
HEAD White, with greyish patch or streak behind eye, often extending over rear crown.
BODY Very pale grey clouding confined to lower hindneck and breast-sides.
WINGS Clear-cut black wing-tip (in some lights showing little contrast with rest of wing) extending to 5th or 6th primary; obvious white tips from 3rd or 4th increasing in size inwards. Outer one or two greater primary coverts sometimes with some black.
TAIL White.
BARE PARTS Bill black or blackish-brown, usually with small red line near tip of culmen and sometimes also near tip of gonys. Legs blackish or grey.

Adult summer/third-summer (Fig. 20E) Acquired by head and body moult, February to April. *As adult winter except:*
HEAD Slaty-black hood fully developed. Prominent white crescents above and posteriorly below eye.
BODY Neck and underparts white.
WINGS White primary tips reduced or lacking.
BARE PARTS Iris dark brown. Orbital ring, mouth and gape red. Bill dull red or clouded with blackish subterminally, often with bright orange-red or scalet tip. Legs dull red or blackish-brown.

Franklin's Gull
Larus pipixcan

(Figs. 12D and 22, Photographs 131–157)

Adult summer

IDENTIFICATION

   This highly migratory and distinctive small gull is unlikely to be confused with any other species except Laughing Gull: both are vagrants to Europe from America.

   Franklin's is, on average, slightly smaller than Black-headed and Laughing Gulls. On the ground and in flight its outline is reminiscent of the smaller Little Gull, lacking the long-winged silhouette of Laughing Gull. The bill can look rather stout, but it lacks the long, drooping shape which is usually striking on Laughing Gull. It is also proportionately shorter-legged than Laughing. Like Laughing Gull, the grey on the upperparts is very dark, close to that of the British subspecies of Lesser Black-backed Gull *L. fuscus graellsii*. In winter and first-year plumages, Franklin's has a diagnostic blackish 'half-hood', covering the ear-coverts, rear crown and nape (thus much more extensive than on other hooded gulls in winter plumage which, however, may show a similar pattern at transitional stages of moult to or from summer plumage), with strikingly thick, white crescents above and below the eye which usually meet at the rear.

   As well as the size and structural differences, first-winters differ from Laughing Gulls of the same age in having the half-hood, almost wholly white underparts without the extensive grey breast-band and flanks, small white tips to most of the primaries in fresh plumage, mainly grey inner primaries, mainly whitish underwing coverts, and thinner black tail band which does not extend to the all-white outer pair of feathers. First-summers and second-years are less readily separable from second-year and adult Laughing Gulls, but the half-hood in winter, the thicker white crescents above and

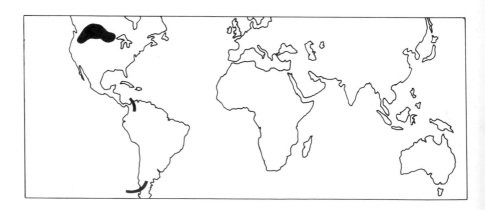

Fig. 21.   World distribution of **Franklin's Gull** *Larus pipixcan*, showing approximate breeding range (solid black) and approximate limits of winter/non-breeding range (black line). Rare vagrant to Europe; in Britain, up to 1980, six records since first in 1970.

below the eye which usually meet at the rear, the prominently white-tipped primaries (obvious when perched), and the grey-centred tail, as well as the size and structural differences, are the best distinctions. When fully adult, further differences are the distinctive wing pattern, usually pink-flushed underparts, and the diagnostic grey-centred tail, the latter unique among adult gulls.

Unlike any other gull, Franklin's has a complete moult in both spring and autumn. As with other gulls, however, the post-juvenile moult (from fledging to October) to first-winter plumage involves only the head and body feathers, and usually also some coverts of the inner wing which reduces the extent of the brown carpal-bar. The first complete moult takes place in winter quarters from January to April, from first-winter to first-summer plumage, and subsequent moults are always complete, in autumn prior to the southward migration (from July to October) to winter plumage, and in 'spring' prior to the northward migration (from November to April) to summer plumage. A very few museum specimens of first-years, however, appear not to fit into this moult pattern, suggesting that some first-winter individuals miss the complete moult to first-summer, or have only a partial one.

Fig. 22 shows the typical appearance of the various ages, but there is much individual variation, and winter observations in South America show that it is difficult to age with certainty the majority of second-winter/adult winter individuals in the field. Individuals showing a wing pattern similar or close to that of Fig. 22D are certain second-winters, and those with wing patterns like 22E or 22F are adult, but there is every intergradation between these extremes, and it would seem safest to assign such intermediate examples as 'adult or second-winter'. Individual variation of adult wing pattern is from that of 22D to that of 22F.

I am indebted to E. J. Mackrill, whose expert analysis of the field situation which he has observed in North and South America, and whose extensive series of superb photographs of Franklin's Gulls, have been a major contribution to this summary and to the detailed descriptions.

AGEING SUMMARY

Juvenile: scaly brown mantle and scapulars (summer to October).

First-winter: half-hood, uniform grey mantle and scapulars, brown on coverts of inner wing, and blackish primaries, secondary bar and tail band (August to February).

First-summer: half-hood as first-winter (or hood partially developed); grey mantle, scapulars, and inner wing; no complete white division between grey of primaries and black wing-tip; black extensive on outer two or three primaries, often extending strongly onto greater primary coverts and alula; and sometimes an indistinct partial secondary bar or tail band (February to September).

Second-winter: as adult winter, but black on outer primaries extending up outer webs, with little or no white division from grey of primary bases. Many probably inseparable from adult winter in the field, but those with this wing-tip pattern are certain second-winters (August to February).

Adult summer/second-summer: as adult winter, but full black hood (February to September).

Adult winter/third-winter: half-hood; uniform grey upperparts and inner wing; obvious white division between grey of primaries and black on wing-tip; black on wing-tip less extensive than on typical second-winter, with large mirror on first primary and very large white tips to all outer primaries. Many probably inseparable from second-winter in the field, but those with this wing-tip pattern are certain adults (August to February).

DETAILED DESCRIPTIONS

Juvenile (not illustrated, but wing and tail pattern similar to first-winter, Figs. 12D, 22A and 22B)
HEAD Forehead, lores, chin, throat and crescents above and below eye whitish. Eye-crescent, ear-coverts, rear crown and nape mainly uniform dark grey-brown, more streaked on crown and nape, forming clear-cut half-hood.
BODY Underparts and rump white, breast-sides faintly washed brown. Hindneck, mantle, scapulars and back brownish; scapulars fringed pale giving indistinct scaly pattern.
WINGS Carpal-bar brownish with pale fringes. Greater coverts mainly uniform brownish-grey. Secondaries grey-brown with blackish centres (forming secondary bar) and prominent white tips forming white trailing edge to inner wing. Outer primaries, their coverts, and alula mainly black, with grey on outer webs increasing inwards from 3rd or 4th, and black decreasing to subterminal band on 6th or 7th. Small white tips on outer primaries increasing in size inwards to 5th or 6th, remainder with prominent white fringes at tips. Greater under primary coverts prominently marked with dusky, remainder of underwing coverts mainly white.
TAIL Mainly pale grey, with black subterminal band, broadest in centre and not extending to outer pair of feathers, which are all-white.
BARE PARTS Bill blackish, sometimes a shade paler at base. Legs blackish.

First-winter (Fig 12D, 22A and 22B) Acquired by post-juvenile head and body moult, which often also includes more or less of the coverts of the inner wing, summer to October. *As juvenile except:*
HEAD Half-hood blackish-brown, with thick white crescents above and below eyes, usually joining at rear.
BODY Breast-sides faintly washed grey. Underparts sometimes pink-flushed. Back brownish. Hindneck, mantle and scapulars clear dark grey; scapulars occasionally with fine brown shaft-streaks.
WINGS Brown areas becoming faded paler, and pale tertial fringes and small white tips on outer primaries reduced or lacking.
BARE PARTS Bill black, often brownish at base. Legs black to reddish-brown.

First-summer (Fig. 22C) Acquired by complete moult, January to April.
HEAD Pattern as first-winter, but often blackish: hood partially developed on a few individuals. Thick white crescents above and below eye, meeting at rear.
BODY Mantle, back and scapulars uniform dark grey, remainder white; underparts sometimes with pale pink flush.
WINGS Dark grey, with broad white trailing edge on secondaries and inner primaries. Outer five or six primaries with neat white tips increasing in size inwards. Black on outer five or six primaries decreasing in extent inwards to subterminal mark on 5th or 6th, extensive on outer webs of outer two or three. Outer greater primary

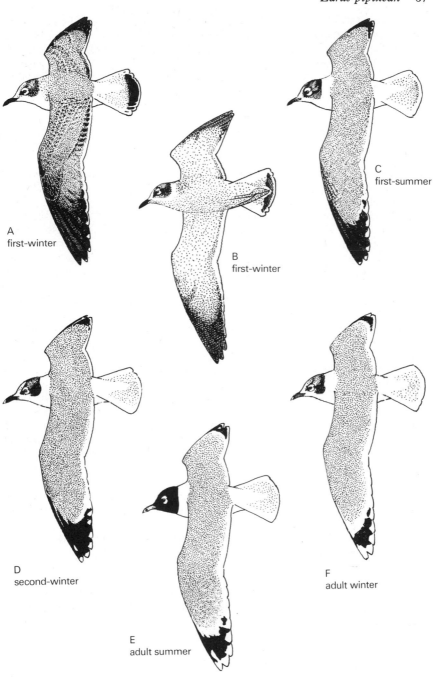

A
first-winter

B
first-winter

C
first-summer

D
second-winter

E
adult summer

F
adult winter

Fig. 22. **Franklin's Gulls** *Larus pipixcan* in flight.

coverts brownish with dark centres, and alula often blackish: these dark markings form a dusky extension of the black wing-tip up leading edge of outer wing, which may be difficult to discern in the field. Variable number of secondaries have dark centres, sometimes forming indistinct partial secondary bar.

TAIL Terminal fringe and sides white, with grey centrally sometimes becoming darker towards tip, and occasionally also with dark subterminal spots forming indistinct partial tail band.

BARE PARTS Bill and legs blackish, or bill reddish at base.

A few individuals apparently miss the complete moult to first-summer, or have only a partial one.

Second-winter (Fig. 22D) Acquired by complete moult, July to October. *As first-summer except:*

HEAD Half-hood like first winter, but blacker.

BODY Underparts often pink-flushed.

WINGS Black on primaries less extensive, with complete black outer web only on 1st, and subterminal black bands on 3rd to 5th, and sometimes subterminal black spot on 6th. Small area of white divides black on 3rd to 6th from grey bases. Outer primaries usually with obvious white tips increasing in size inwards to 5th or 6th, and 1st often with small mirror on inner web near tip. Outer greater primary coverts grey, sometimes with indistinct dusky centres or shaft streaks. No secondary bar.

TAIL White terminal fringe and sides, grey centrally.

BARE PARTS Bill blackish or brownish, with red or orange at tip. Legs blackish or dull red. Eye and orbital ring dark.

Adult summer/second-summer (Fig. 22E) Acquired by complete moult, November to April.

HEAD Full slaty-black hood, with thick white crescents or oval patches posteriorly above and below eye, joining at rear.

BODY As first-summer, with pink flush on underparts.

WINGS As second-winter, except black usually less extensive, sometimes barely extending to 5th primary and divided from grey remainder by broad band of white across primaries. Larger white primary tips than on second-winter. Pattern of black variable (typical variations shown in Figs. 22E and 22F): some may have more black, little different from second-winter, except black not extending up outer webs of outermost primaries. When perched, black on wing-tip surrounded by white.

TAIL As second-winter.

BARE PARTS Bill red, usually with dark subterminal marks or thin band. Mouth and gape scarlet. Legs red. Orbital ring rich pink.

Adult winter/third-winter (Fig. 22F) Acquired by complete moult, July to October. As second-winter except wing pattern as adult summer, and bare parts often generally redder, and bill usually with red or orange at extreme tip, or reddish with black subterminal mark.

Audouin's, Herring, Lesser Black-backed, Great Black-backed and Great Black-headed Gulls

The five species covered here are grouped because of their large size and similarity especially in juvenile and first-year plumages. Glaucous *Larus hyperboreus* and Iceland Gulls *L. glaucoides* (Group 5) are the only other western Palearctic species of similar size, but are readily separated from this group by the lack of black or brown on wings and tail at all ages.

The identification of juveniles and first-years is often difficult, requiring reasonable views and practice. Some adult coloration is usually acquired on the mantle and scapulars during the second year, making identification easier, but in these and even in third-year and adult plumages the separation of the two similar pairs (Herring *L. argentatus*/Audouin's *L. audouinii*, and Lesser Black-backed *L. fuscus*/Great Black-backed *L. marinus*) remains difficult at long range.

The ageing of large gulls is less straightforward than is generally the case for smaller species: the longer period of immaturity gives a potential for individual plumage variation which increases with each successive moult. Juveniles, first-winters and first-summers can generally be aged with certainty, mainly because the retained juvenile wings and tail have a relatively standard pattern. There is, however, an

---

Table 3: Measurements (mm) of five gulls Larus *(from Dwight 1925)*

	sample	wing	tail	bill	tarsus
Audouin's Gull *L. audouinii*	8	370–402	138–158	43–53	52–60
Herring Gull *L. argentatus argentatus/argenteus*	18	375–447	152–189	45–58	55–70
Lesser Black-backed Gull *L. fuscus*	36	382–438	142–169	44–56	57–69
Great Black-backed Gull *L. marinus*	15	454–498	181–211	57–72	72–85
Great Black-headed Gull *L. ichthyaetus*	17	422–500	171–203	50–65	65–83

---

overlap in the appearance of a few advanced second-years and retarded third-years, and a much greater overlap between advanced third-years and retarded fourth-years and older. The transition from the mainly dull-coloured juvenile bill to full adult coloration is similarly variable: first-years have a relatively standard bill colour and pattern, but second- and third-years display great variation, generally of little help to ageing.

It is usually believed that large gulls typically acquire adult plumage in their fourth winter, but it is well known that some may still show traces of immaturity at that age or even subsequently. Monaghan & Duncan (1979) described three breeding Herring Gulls, ringed as nestlings and known to be in their fourth summer: one was adult (as would be expected at that age), but two had extensive dark markings on the outer greater primary coverts and alula, and a faint tail band, features usually considered to indicate third-year plumage. It seems likely that all large gulls—not only Herring Gulls—may be subject to similar variation. It should thus be borne in mind that the illustrations and descriptions of immatures given for this group represent what are thought to be typical examples. In practice, the ageing, at least of individuals with plumage intermediate between those described for second- and third-years, and all those with plumage resembling that described for third-years, should be tentative: use of such terms as 'second-or third-summer' and 'third-year type' is suggested to describe them.

More information based on ringed birds of known age is needed to ascertain the extent of variation in the length of immaturity and varying appearance at different ages of large gulls.

In summer, when a combination of worn, faded plumage and the start of the complete autumn moult frequently produces a generally nondescript appearance, the ageing of immature large gulls may be particularly difficult, although detailed examination of the patterns of adjacent new and old primaries (on trapped birds, for example) can provide extra clues to age.

Herring (Fig. 26), Lesser Black-backed (Fig. 28) and Great Black-backed Gulls (Fig. 30)—in order of descending general abundance—are familiar in most of the western Palearctic. Immatures provide an identification challenge, and more attention to flocks of large gulls—and familiarisation with the identification of immatures—could lead to further European records of Audouin's (Fig. 24) and Great Black-headed Gulls *L. ichthyaetus* (Fig. 32), and a more complete knowledge of their status within their known ranges.

The subspecies of Herring and Lesser Black-backed Gulls are discussed and described under 'Geographical variation' after the detailed descriptions. While typical examples are identifiable in the field, there is a good deal of intergradation in appearance, and caution is advisable in assigning individuals to a particular subspecies outside its usual range.

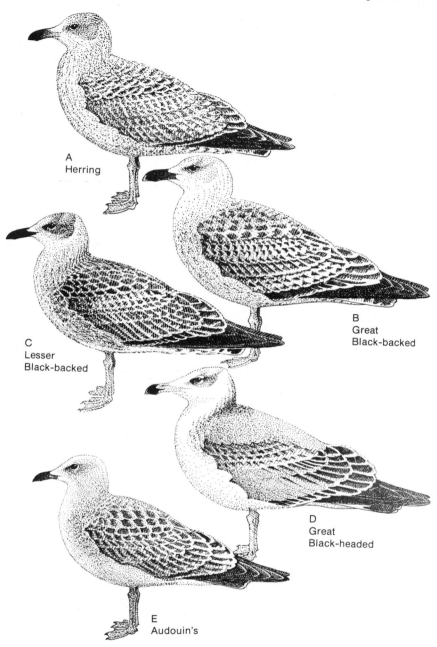

A
Herring

B
Great
Black-backed

C
Lesser
Black-backed

D
Great
Black-headed

E
Audouin's

Fig. 23.   First-winter **Herring** *Larus argentatus*, **Great Black-backed** *L. marinus*, **Lesser Black-backed** *L. fuscus*, **Great Black-headed** *L. ichthyaetus* and **Audouin's Gulls** *L. audouinii*, showing comparative sizes, shapes and stances.

Audouin's Gull
Larus audouinii

(Figs. 23E and 25, Photographs 158–169)

Adult summer

IDENTIFICATION

This rare Mediterranean speciality typically frequents wave-washed rocky coasts and islands, and—especially away from the breeding areas—flat, sandy shores. Adults (mainly in winter) and immatures—presumably from west Mediterranean breeding colonies—occur on the Atlantic coast of northwest Africa, especially Morocco (Smith 1972): it has been recorded in Portugal, and vagrants, especially immatures which are apparently less specialised in their feeding habits than adults (Garcia 1977), could occur farther north.

At all ages, differences of structure and behaviour are among the best distinctions from Herring Gull. Audouin's is only slightly smaller, but obviously slimmer and more elegant. It is a graceful flier, the slimmer wings and shorter, square-cut tail (usually held closely folded and straight) give a 'sail plane' appearance. It glides more, often for very long distances, on gently-arched wings, and performs agile swoops and turns. It is exclusively a marine feeder, picking from the surface with a lunge of its bill and long neck, or plunging more deeply into the sea from a low-level glide, often with a distinctive 'buck' of its tail as it enters the water. It is not an aggressive scavenger like other large gulls. It lacks Herring Gull's fierce expression, having a smaller, slimmer head with a sloping, elongated forehead giving a marked 'snout' effect and peaking well behind the eye. When alert, the neck is long and slender, and its stance more upright than Herring Gull. The bill is shorter and deeper, and is often held 'drooping' downwards when perched.

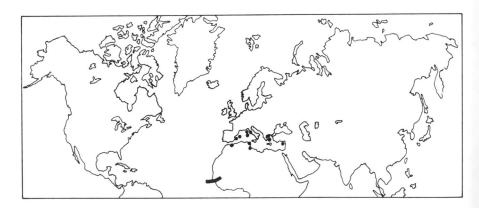

Fig. 24.   World distribution of **Audouin's Gull** *Larus audouinii*, showing breeding areas (black spots). The winter/non-breeding range extends out of the Mediterranean, mainly to the Atlantic coast of Morocco; the black line indicates the approximate southern limit. Vagrant north to Portugal.

Herring Gulls of the Mediterranean race *L. a. michahellis* (p. 85) are a potential source of confusion to observers new to the Mediterranean, because their plumage, especially of immatures, is markedly different from that of the north European subspecies. Once aware of this pitfall, however, there should be little difficulty in identifying Audouin's.

Juvenile Audouin's is described by Garcia (1977): compared with Herring Gull of the same age, it is generally darker, with smooth grey-brown head (without obviously darker ear-coverts) and underparts, and a suffused whitish 'face' and contrasting whitish crown. The upperparts are darker, with neat, pale feather edgings, forming a more striking scaly pattern. The upperwing has two uniform dark bars—a secondary bar and another across the greater coverts—unlike Herring Gull, which has only a secondary bar; the inner primaries are only slightly paler than the blackish outer ones; thus, it lacks the prominent pale window, obvious from above and below on Herring Gull. The underwing has contrasting dark and light bars on the coverts; this area is paler and more uniform on Herring Gull. The tail and rump patterns are quite different from those of Herring Gull: apart from the white terminal fringe, the tail is wholly dark, contrasting with the mainly white undertail-coverts and the distinctively U-shaped white rump. The legs are dark grey, whereas Herring Gull's are pinkish.

Most of the juvenile differences are also found in first-winter and first-summer plumages, although, after the autumn and spring partial moults, the head and body become generally whiter than on Herring Gull, and the wings and tail become much worn and faded by the first summer. First-year Lesser Black-backed Gulls have a similar upperwing pattern: at long range they are probably best distinguished by their darker head and body, rather uniformly dark underwing and more cleary banded tail.

Second-years differ from Herring Gulls of the same age by having paler grey upperparts (especially compared with the rather dark grey of the Mediterranean subspecies), neater, thinner tail band, more clear-cut white primary tips (visible only when perched, but liable to disappear through wear), dark legs and usually reddish-based bill.

Third-years and adults, when seen well, bear no more than a passing resemblance to Herring Gulls. At long range, perhaps the best distinctions of Audouin's are the black-looking bill and legs, lack of prominent white mirrors in the black wing-tip, paler grey upperparts, lack of prominent white leading and trailing edges to the inner wing, and the different flight and feeding behaviour. At close range, the grey mantle colour extends onto the rump and as a diagnostic faint suffusion on the hindneck, flanks, belly and underwing. The black wing-tip has only one small mirror, often lacking on third-years, difficult to see except at close range from below. When perched, the white scapular- and tertial-crescents are very faint. The bill is deep red, with an ill-defined black subterminal band and yellowish tip: the latter is often invisible, accentuating the stubby shape.

In winter, third-year and adult Audouin's apparently have a white head, lacking the dark streaking acquired by most other large gulls in winter (thus, there is apparently little difference between summer and winter plumages). The Mediterranean race of Herring Gull, however, has a mainly white head in winter, unlike that of the north European subspecies.

AGEING SUMMARY (see general discussion on ageing large gulls on pp. 69–70)

Juvenile: smooth grey-brown head and underparts, striking scaly pattern on upperparts. Primaries, secondaries and tail mainly blackish. Bill mainly black (summer to October).

First-winter: as juvenile, except head and underparts probably less smooth grey-brown, and upperparts less neatly scaled (September to April).

First-summer: as first-winter, except head and underparts mainly white, wings and tail much worn and faded. Upperparts less scaly, paler (March to October).

Second-winter: faint dusky head markings, upperparts and coverts of inner wing mainly grey. Blackish outer primaries and coverts, secondary bar and tail band. Bill base usually dark red (August to April).

Second-summer: as second-winter, except head white, and wings and tail much worn and faded (March to October).

Third-winter: as adult, except much black on outer greater primary coverts, and sometimes a trace of a tail band (August to April).

Third-summer: as third-winter, except primary tips reduced or lacking through wear (March to October).

Adult winter/fourth-winter: black on wing-tip confined to primaries (August to April).

Adult summer/fourth-summer: as adult winter, except white primary tips reduced or lacking through wear (March to October).

DETAILED DESCRIPTIONS

Juvenile (Fig. 25A. From below and when perched, similar to first-winter, 25B and 23E)
HEAD Smooth uniform grey-brown (lacking obviously darker ear-coverts) and with whitish or creamy face, crown and nape: white-capped effect often prominent. Dusky eye-crescent and thin white crescents above and below eye.
BODY Underparts smooth grey-brown, belly, vent and undertail-coverts white, latter with dark marks. Lower hindneck, back, mantle and most of rump grey-brown, with subtle scaly effect, remainder of rump and uppertail-coverts forming distinctively U-shaped white area contrasting with dark tail. Scapulars dark brown, with neat pale fringes, forming prominent scaly pattern.
WINGS Median and lesser coverts and tertials scaly like scapulars: remainder of wing blackish, inner primaries only slightly paler than remainder, with black subterminal marks. Greater coverts and secondaries blackish, with fine white fringes. Underwing has prominent dark and light bars across coverts.
TAIL Mainly black, with white terminal fringe: base greyish, with little or no white.
BARE PARTS Iris dark. Bill black, sometimes flesh-coloured at base. Legs dark grey.

First-winter (Figs. 23E and 25B, wings and tail similar to juvenile, 25A) Acquired

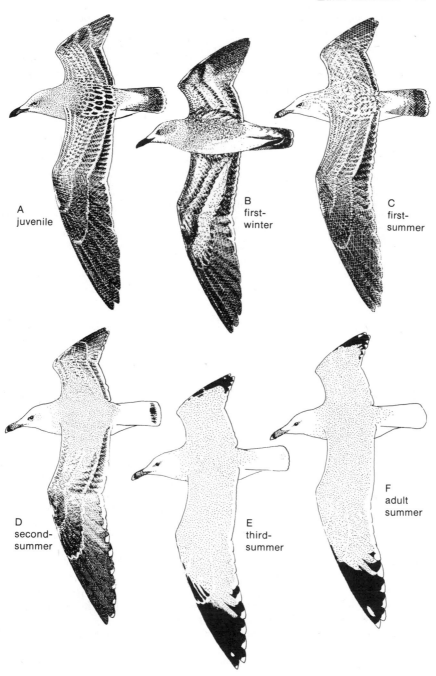

Fig. 25. Audouin's Gull *Larus audouinii* in flight.

by post-juvenile head and body moult during autumn, probably complete by September to November.

Apparently as juvenile, except head and underparts probably less smooth grey-brown; scapulars less scaled; bill tipped whitish.

First-summer (Fig. 25C, underwing and tail similar to first-winter, 25B) Acquired by head and body moult, probably February to April.

As first-winter, except head and underparts mainly white, latter with dark streaks and smudges; wings and tail becoming much worn and faded, especially median and lesser coverts, which become more uniform, brownish; mantle and scapulars paler, probably with some clear grey; bill paler, with blackish tip or subterminal band.

Second-winter (not illustrated, but similar to second-summer, Fig. 25D) Acquired by complete moult, probably June to October.

HEAD White with dusky eye-crescent and faint streaking.

BODY Underparts and rump white. Mantle, back and scapulars uniform pale grey.

WINGS Blackish secondary bar; remainder of inner wing mainly clear grey, with brown markings on coverts of variable extent. Inner primaries mainly clear grey, remainder of outer wing mainly blackish; all except outer one or two primaries and their coverts with neat white tips in fresh plumage. Underwing mainly white, with a few dark markings on coverts.

TAIL White, with neat black subterminal band.

BARE PARTS As first-summer, except base of bill often reddish.

Second-summer (Fig. 25D) Acquired by head and body moult, probably February to April.

As second-winter, except head white; dark areas on upperwing much faded, browner; more clear grey on inner wing-coverts; white primary tips often lacking through wear; base of bill usually dark red; orbital ring red.

Third-winter (not illustrated, but similar to third-summer, Fig. 25E) Acquired by complete moult, probably June to October. Some may acquire adult plumage at this age, but probably the majority take an extra year. *As adult winter, except*:

WINGS Extensive black on outer greater primary coverts, sometimes extending onto alula, giving prominent 'headlights' effect on leading edge of outer wing in flight. Mirror on outer primary tiny or lacking.

TAIL Sometimes with faint dark subterminal marks.

Third-summer (Fig. 25E) Acquired by head and body moult, probably February to April. As third-winter, except white primary tips reduced or lacking through wear.

Adult winter/fourth-winter (not illustrated, but similar to adult summer, Fig. 25F) Acquired by complete moult, probably June to October.

HEAD White. Hindneck, nape and sometimes crown with grey wash extending from mantle.

BODY Underparts washed pale grey, but contrast with white head visible only in dull light at close range. Upperparts smooth, pale pearly-grey (similar in colour to upperparts of Black-headed Gull *L. ridibundus*) shading onto rump, thus no sharp division between back and rump.

WINGS Grey, as upperparts, even paler on outer wing because of diffuse whiter fringes to coverts and inner primaries. When perched indistinct white scapular- and tertial-crescents, invisible at long range. Inner wing with very thin white leading edge and diffuse, indistinct white trailing edge. Black confined to outer primaries, decreasing in extent inwards to small, isolated subterminal spots on 5th and 6th, forming clear-cut black wing tip above and below; remainder of underwing pale grey, secondaries and inner primaries very translucent. Some individuals have small blackish marks on outer two or three greater primary coverts, not as extensive as on typical third-years, and may be adult. Outer primaries prominently tipped white, usually visible only when perched. Small, round, white mirror in inner web of outer primary, visible only at close range from below.

TAIL White, often with grey wash at bases of central feathers.

BARE PARTS Iris brown, orbital ring, mouth and gape red. Bill deep coral-red, looking black at ranges of 100 m or more, with single or double black subterminal band and yellowish tip, the latter often invisible at long range. Legs dull greyish or olive, soles yellow.

Adult summer/fourth-summer (Fig. 25F) Acquired by head and body moult, probably February to May.

As adult winter, except white primary tips reduced or lacking through wear, and red at base of bill perhaps darker, more often appearing wholly blackish at long range.

Herring Gull
Larus argentatus
(Figs. 23A and 27, Photographs 170–199)

Second-summer

The identification summary, detailed descriptions and Figs. 23A and 27 refer to the west European subspecies *L. a. argenteus*: the complex racial taxonomy of Herring Gulls, and the distinctions of the other subspecies, are discussed under geographical variation on page 84.

IDENTIFICATION

Herring Gull is on average 20–30% smaller and proportionately less heavily built than Great Black-backed Gull. It is slightly larger than Lesser Black-backed Gull, but with heavier general build and proportionately shorter legs; the wings are proportionately broader and shorter, giving a heavier appearance in flight and a noticeably less attenuated rear-end when perched.

In juvenile, first-winter and first-summer plumages, Herring, Lesser Black-backed and Great Black-backed Gulls have a basically similar pattern and coloration. The appearance and specific differences of juveniles are described in Table 4, and those of first-winter and first-summer plumages in the detailed descriptions. At these ages, some of the distinctions involve rather subtle comparisons of colour tones and

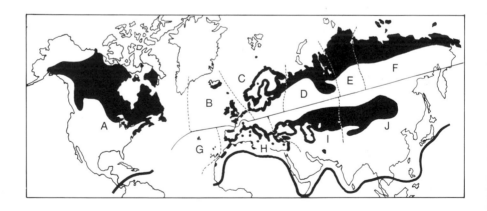

Fig. 26.   World distribution of **Herring Gull** *Larus argentatus*, showing approximate breeding range (solid black) and approximate southern limit of winter/non-breeding range (thick black line). The thin line marks the division between the northern or nominate '*argentatus*' group of subspecies and the southern '*cachinnans*' group: the dotted lines mark the approximate breeding ranges of the subspecies. (A) *L. a. smithsonianus*; (B) *L. a. argenteus*; (C) *L. a. argentatus*; (D) *L. a. heuglini*; (E) *L. a. taimyrensis*; (F) *L. a. vegae*; (G) *L. a. atlantis*; (H) *L. a. michahellis*; (I) *L. a. cachinnans*; (J) *L. a. mongolicus*. The geographical variation of Herring Gulls is discussed on pages 84–87.

patterns (which in themselves are subject to a good deal of individual variation), and they may not be readily discernible until after a good deal of careful study of mixed flocks containing two or all three species.

In second-year plumages, Herring Gull has generally pale upperparts (usually with extensive clear grey at least on the mantle and scapulars) reflecting the eventual adult coloration, and thus is readily separable from the black-backed pair, both of which are obviously dark-backed at these ages.

Third-years and adults are readily identifiable: Audouin's (p. 72) and Great Black-headed Gulls (p. 88) are the only other pale grey-backed large gulls with black on the primaries, and Glaucous and Iceland Gulls have all-white wing-tips. The best long range distinctions from the similar but much smaller Common Gull *L. canus* are described on page 44.

AGEING SUMMARY (see general discussion on ageing large gulls on pp. 69–70)

Juvenile: whole plumage fresh and unworn. Head and underparts rather uniformly streaked grey-brown. Neat scaly pattern on mantle, uniformly barred wing coverts. Bill blackish, with diffuse pale base (summer to October).

First-winter: as juvenile except head and sometimes underparts generally whiter. Barred pattern on upperparts more irregular, less scaly (September to March).

First-summer: as first-winter, except head and underparts generally whitish, barred upperparts paler, wings and tail becoming much worn and faded (March to September).

Second-winter: extensive dusky streaking on head, usually some clear grey on mantle and scapulars. Outer primaries and secondary bar blackish, inner primaries and coverts of inner wing generally greyish, the latter with variable amount of brown. Extensive blackish tail band, not as extensive as on first-years. Underwing mainly whitish. Bill extensively pale at base (September to March).

Second-summer: as second-winter, except head and underparts mainly white, mantle and scapulars uniform pale grey or with few brown feathers. Wings and tail becoming much worn and faded (March to September).

Third-winter: as adult winter, except much black on outer coverts of outer wing and alula, black wing-tip less clear cut and lacking prominent mirrors, usually some brown freckling on coverts of inner wing and tertials, faint tail band, black subterminal band or small mark on bill (September to April).

Third-summer: as third-winter, except head white, wings and tail faded, and white primary tips reduced or lacking through wear (February to September).

Adult winter/fourth-winter: extensive dusky head markings, upperparts and wings uniform pale grey, black wing-tip clear-cut and confined to outer primaries, two prominent mirrors, tail white, no black on bill (September to March).

Adult summer/fourth-summer: as adult winter, except head white, and white primary tips reduced or lacking through wear (February to September).

Table 4: Detailed descriptions of juvenile **Herring** L. argentatus, **Lesser Black-backed**
L. fuscus *and* **Great Black-backed Gulls** L. marinus

The specific differences are in italics: some of the distinctions involve rather subtle comparisons of colour tones and patterns (which in themselves are subject to a good deal of individual variation), and they may not be apparent until after a good deal of careful study of mixed flocks containing two or all three species

	Herring Gull (Fig. 27A. When perched—except mantle and scapulars— and from below, similar to first-winter, 23A and 27B)	Lesser Black-backed Gull (Fig. 29A. When perched and from below, similar to first-winter, 23C and 29B)	Great Black-backed Gull (Fig. 31A. When perched and from below, similar to first-winter, 23B and 31B)
Head and underparts	Streaked grey-brown with paler face and nape, darker ear-coverts and blackish eye-crescent. *Generally paler than Lesser Black-backed*	Streaked dark grey-brown with paler face and nape, prominent dark ear-patch and blackish eye-crescent; blackish mottling on breast-sides and flanks, belly paler. *Generally darker than Herring with coarser markings*	Streaked grey-brown with prominent blackish eye-crescent, but *head and upper breast contrastingly whiter than rest of underparts*, which are generally more coarsely streaked than on Herring and Lesser Black-backed
Mantle and scapulars	Feathers grey-brown, with pale edgings forming *slightly paler, less contrasting scaly pattern than Lesser Black-backed* and lacking strongly chequered pattern of Great Black-backed	*Darker than Herring, scaly pattern more contrasting*	Feathers blackish, with broad whitish edges, forming *contrasting chequered pattern*, less scaly than Herring and Lesser Black-backed, and generally paler than latter
Rump	Streaked grey-brown, general tone as mantle and scapulars and base of tail, thus *contrast usually slight*	Generally whitish with darker streaking, *contrastingly paler than mantle and scapulars*	Similar to Lesser Black-backed
Coverts of inner wing	General coloration as mantle and scapulars, but pattern more barred, less scaly, including *outer greater coverts which lack the uniform dark bar of Lesser Black-backed*	General coloration as mantle and scapulars, but pattern more barred, less scaly; *outer greater coverts mainly blackish-brown forming 'extra' dark bar on inner upperwing*, lacking on Herring and Great Black-backed	General coloration as mantle and scapulars, but pattern more barred, less chequered; generally paler than Lesser Black-backed, like Herring in tone and pattern, *but more contrast*
Secondaries	Mainly blackish-brown, forming secondary bar	As Herring	As Herring
Outer wing	Mainly blackish-brown, but inner primaries pale (with dark subterminal marks) forming *pale window, prominent from above and below*	Almost wholly blackish; inner primaries slightly paler than remainder and secondaries, thus *lacking prominent pale window*	Pattern intermediate between Herring and Lesser Black-backed; *window effect in some lights*, not as prominent as on Herring

(*Table 4 cont.*)

	Herring Gull (Fig. 27A. When perched—except mantle and scapulars— and from below, similar to first-winter, 23A and 27B)	Lesser Black-backed Gull (Fig. 29A. When perched and from below, similar to first-winter, 23C and 29B)	Great Black-backed Gull (Fig. 31A. When perched and from below, similar to first-winter, 23B and 31B)
Underwing	*Prominent pale window, remainder rather uniform pale grey-brown*	Window effect very slight or lacking, generally dark, rather uniform blackish-brown	Slight window effect; coverts rather uniform blackish-brown, remainder grey-brown giving *rather subtle two-tone effect*
Tail	Base whitish with darker bars, generally grey-brown as rump and upperparts, thus broad, blackish-brown subterminal band less contrasting than on Lesser Black-backed, and lacking distinctive 'watered' pattern of Great Black-backed	Base typically rather whiter than on Herring, with thin black bars on outer feathers, *blackish subterminal band usually more contrasting, solidly blackish and clear-cut*	Base generally whiter than on Herring. *Blackish subterminal band typically highly diffuse and broken, forming distinctive 'watered' pattern*
Bare parts	Iris dark brown. Bill blackish with usually *prominent diffuse pale area at base,* mainly on lower mandible. Legs dull flesh	Iris dark brown. *Bill black without pale base.* Legs dull flesh	Iris dark brown. *Bill wholly black except for small whitish area at tip; large size emphasised by sharp contrast with whitish head.* Legs dull flesh

DETAILED DESCRIPTIONS (These refer to the west European race *L. a. argenteus*: for difference of other races see pp. 84–87)

Juvenile See Table 4.

First-winter (Figs. 23A and 27B, wings and tail similar to juvenile, 27A) Acquired by post-juvenile head and body moult, July to November.

Appearance and identification as for juvenile, except head (and sometimes underparts) whiter, less uniform, and mantle and scapulars less scaly with more complex pattern of dark bars. Generally paler than Lesser Black-backed, even more than in juvenile plumage.

First-summer (Fig. 27C, underwing and tail similar to first-winter, 27B) Acquired by head and body moult, January to April.

Appearance and identification as for juvenile, except head and underparts often extensively whitish. Dark areas on wings and tail often faded to pale brown, and pale areas faded to whitish, giving generally very pale appearance by summer, strikingly paler than first-summer Lesser Black-backed. A few clear grey scapulars may be acquired during April. Bill often extensively pale at base. Iris sometimes slightly paler.

Second-winter (not illustrated, but wings and tail similar to second-summer, Fig. 27D) Acquired by complete moult, May to October.

HEAD White with usually extensive dusky streaking.

BODY Underparts and rump mainly white, with variable amount of dark streaking. Mantle and scapulars similar to first-winter, but usually with much clear grey.

WINGS Outer wing mainly blackish, but inner four primaries and their coverts mainly clear grey, thus window more clear-cut and contrasting than on first-years. Coverts of inner wing paler, sometimes with much clear grey, more uniform than on first-years, with variable amount of brown mottling; prominent blackish-brown secondary bar. Underwing generally whiter than on first-year.

TAIL Extensively whitish at base; extensive blackish subterminal band.

BARE PARTS Iris often becoming pale. Bill usually extensively flesh or yellowish-flesh, with dark subterminal area and sometimes some reddish on gonys, but pattern and colour highly variable. Legs dull flesh.

Second-summer (Fig. 27D) Acquired by head and body moult, January to April.

As second-winter, except head and underparts mainly white. Mantle and scapulars clear grey, sometimes with a few brown-barred feathers. Dark areas on wings and tail faded, and pale areas faded to whitish (often contrasting with grey mantle and scapulars to give saddle effect) by summer. Iris dark or pale. Bill often developing yellowish adult coloration, and sometimes reddish spot on gonys, but usually with extensive dark subterminal area.

Third-winter (Fig. 27E) Acquired by complete moult, June to October.

HEAD AND BODY White with extensive dusky streaking especially around eye and on crown, nape and hindneck; few streaks on breast-sides and flanks. Mantle and scapulars uniform pale grey.

WINGS As adult winter, except black area on wing-tip larger, extending onto greater primary coverts and alula, white primary tips smaller, usually only on mirror (sometimes none), and extensive brown freckling especially on inner greater coverts and tertials. Underwing as adult winter or with some brown marks on coverts.

TAIL White with, usually, faint subterminal band of highly variable extent and pattern.

BARE PARTS Iris pale yellow. Bill colours as adult, but usually generally paler and with dark subterminal mark. Legs bright or pale flesh.

Third-summer (not illustrated, but wings and tail similar to third-winter, Fig. 27E) Acquired by head and body moult, January to April.

As third-winter, except head and underparts usually white, freckled brown areas on inner wings faded to whitish, white primary tips reduced or lacking through wear.

Adult winter/fourth-winter (Fig. 27F) Acquired by complete moult, June to November.

HEAD AND BODY As third-winter.

WINGS Uniform pale grey, black confined to outer primaries, decreasing in extent inwards, usually to small subterminal spot on 6th, forming clear-cut black wing-tip above and below; some individuals also have small blackish marks on outer greater primary coverts. Outer primaries prominently tipped white, usually visible only when perched; mirrors on two outer primaries obvious at long range. Scapular-crescent small or lacking; tertial-crescent prominent when perched. White leading edge to

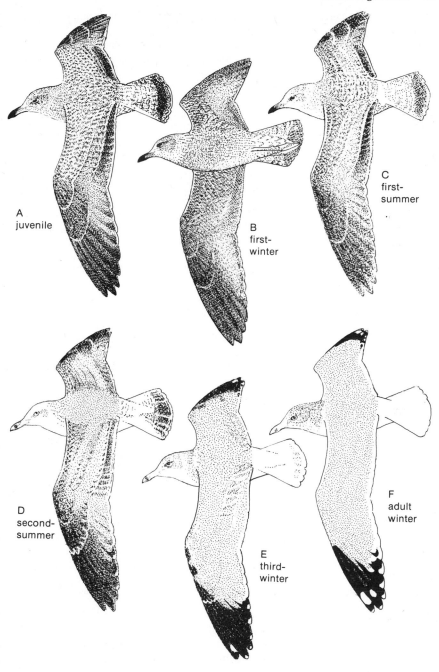

Fig. 27. **Herring Gulls** *Larus argentatus argenteus* in flight.

inner wing indistinct, but trailing edge prominent. Underwing white, with grey subterminal trailing edge and black wing-tip.

BARE PARTS Iris pale yellow. Orbital ring yellow, orange, pink or red. Bill deep or pale yellow, with orange or red spot on gonys and whitish tip; mouth and gape yellow or orange. Legs bright or pale flesh.

Adult summer/fourth-summer (not illustrated, but wings and tail similar to adult winter, Fig. 27F) Acquired by head and body moult, January to April.

As adult winter, except head and underparts white, white primary tips reduced or lacking through wear, and bill and leg colours perhaps generally brighter.

GEOGRAPHICAL VARIATION

The taxonomy of the Herring Gull is notoriously complex. The following summary follows the nomenclature of Vaurie (1965), except for the inclusion of *L. a. argenteus*, following Barth (1975) in a detailed and convincing review of the taxonomy of Herring Gulls in northwestern Europe. The subspecies fall into two fairly distinct groups: the northern or nominate *'argentatus'* group (adults mainly pink-legged except *heuglini*), and the southern or *'cachinnans'* group (adults mainly yellow-legged). Fig. 26 shows the approximate breeding range of each subspecies.

Northern or nominate *'argentatus'* group

L. a. smithsonianus: No western Palearctic records. Averages larger than *argentatus/ argenteus*, wing 397–460 mm (Dwight 1925), first-years perhaps generally darker, with more uniform grey-brown underparts and almost wholly dark tail. Adult upperparts very pale grey, similar to *argenteus*. Legs pink.

L. a. argenteus: Winters in breeding range and south to northern Iberia. Smaller than *argentatus*, slightly larger than Lesser Black-backed Gull. Adult upperparts only slightly darker than Black-headed Gull *L. ridibundus*, with more black on wing-tip and smaller mirrors than *argentatus*. Head and bill rather small compared to *argentatus*. Legs pink.

L. a. argentatus: Winters in breeding range and south to northern Iberia. Averages larger than *argenteus*, some equalling small Great Black-backed Gull. Adults apparently complete the autumn complete moult later than *argenteus*, November to January. Adult upperparts darker than *argenteus*, as dark or slightly darker than Common Gull, with less black on wing-tip and larger white mirrors and tips. Head heavier and more angular, and bill larger and duller (less yellow) in winter. Legs pink or greyish, but yellow-legged adults (often larger and with darker grey upperparts) occur with increasing frequency towards the northeast of breeding range (*'L. a. omissus'* of some authors).

L. a. heuglini: Migrates south to winter in area approximately from Black Sea, Aral Sea, northwest India and Gulf of Aden. Increasing numbers of Herring Gulls wintering in East Africa south to Dar-es-Salaam are thought to be mainly of this subspecies (P. L. Britton *in litt.*). Larger than *argentatus*, wing 410–458 mm (Dwight 1925), and upperparts darker grey than all other subspecies of Herring Gull, similar to palest *L. f. graellsii*. Legs yellow, but readily separated from *L. f. fuscus* in winter range by much larger size and heavier build, slate-grey not blackish upperparts, and usually heavy streaking on hindneck (apparently lacking or faint on *L. f. fuscus*).

L. a. taimyrensis: Winter range not known: Vaurie (1965) suggested Caspian Sea, but this seems unlikely on geographical grounds. Some Herring Gulls wintering in Kenya, paler than *heuglini* with little head-streaking and pale (not pink) to yellow legs, may be this subspecies (P. L. Britton *in litt.*). Adult upperparts intermediate between *heuglini* and *vegae* (thus obviously darker than *argentatus*). As large as *heuglini*, wing 410–453 mm (Dwight 1925), but legs pink or yellow.

L. a. vegae: No western Palearctic records. Winters Japan and coastal China. Adult upperparts paler grey than *taimyrensis*, paler than *mongolicus* (with which it shares at least part of its winter range), and slightly darker than most *argentatus*. Legs pink.

Southern or 'cachinnans' group

L. a. atlantis: Resident; may wander to west African coast. Smaller than *heuglini* and *taimyrensis*, probably similar to *argentatus*, wing 395–428 mm (Dwight 1925), but wings proportionately longer giving sleeker, less bulky general appearance recalling Lesser Black-backed Gull. Adult upperparts between *argentatus* and *L. f. graellsii*, and head apparently heavily streaked in winter giving hooded effect; legs bright-yellow (pink on immatures); adult bill colour bright orange yellow with bright red bill-spot (colour of bill and spot much brighter than on *argenteus/argentatus*); orbital ring red; first-years similar to *michahellis* in general rich brown coloration and defined tail ban (J. van Impe *in litt.*).

L. a. michahellis: Resident within breeding range. Distinctly larger than *atlantis*, wing 435–464 mm (Vaurie 1965), but with similar sleeker, less bulky appearance than *argentatus*. Adult upperparts paler grey than on *atlantis*, but still obviously darker than *argenteus* and most *argentatus*; black on wing-tip extensive as on *argenteus*, with usually prominent mirrors on the outer two primaries (usually only one mirror on *atlantis*); white-headed in winter; bare parts as *atlantis*. Brown areas on immatures generally darker than on *argenteus/argentatus*, with very distinctive rich gingery or rusty tone, fading to gingery-brown. Broad tail band on first-years, more defined than on *argenteus/argentatus*, contrasting with whiter base; bill remains wholly black throughout the first year (perhaps some pale at base by first-summer), lacking the pale base of *argenteus/argentatus*. In summer at least, first-years often have strikingly white head and underparts (unlike *argenteus/argentatus*) contrasting with darker upperparts: this and the black bill give appearance recalling first-year Great Black-backed Gull. Immature *michahellis* looks quite different from *argenteus/argentatus*, and, because of this, observers new to the Mediterranean might mistake it for young Audouin's Gull which is, however, quite different.

L. a. cachinnans: Winters south to eastern Mediterranean, Persian Gulf and northwest India. About same size as *michahellis*, but on average slightly paler and with less black and more white on wing-tip. Apparently mainly white-headed in winter. Bare parts as *atlantis*.

L. a. mongolicus: No western Palearctic records. Winter range not fully known, but includes at least coastal China. Apparently similar to *michahellis* (grey of upperparts darker than pink-legged *vegae*, with which it shares at least part of its winter range). Bare parts as *atlantis*.

There is a good deal of intergradation between subspecies, especially where the breeding ranges adjoin, and individual variation and hybridisation (the latter especially with Glaucous and Lesser Black-backed Gulls in northwestern Europe) are factors which should be borne in mind, as they may sometimes explain the puzzling appearance of a few individuals which apparently fit no known subspecies of Herring Gull. In a detailed field study of winter Herring Gulls in central England, Hume (1978) was able to make a distinction between small, pale *argenteus* (about 90% of the population) and larger, darker *argentatus* (about 10% of the population), although there was more or less intergradation between the two types. A few (about ten individuals) were puzzling: half had extensive white and very restricted black on the wing-tip, while the remainder were small, dark-mantled and white-headed, and had extensive black on the wing-tip and yellow legs. The possibility exists that these were hybrids, the former Herring × Glaucous, although the mantle colour would seem too dark (R. A. Hume *in litt.*), and the latter Herring × Lesser Black-backed, although the white head and the brightness of the yellow legs are characters apparently inconsistent with this view (Hume 1979): it is more likely that the latter were *michahellis/cachinnans*.

Adult Herring Gulls with yellow legs which occur in Britain and northwest Europe are likely to be either *'omissus'*-type *argentatus* from northern Scandinavia (obviously larger and with darker grey upperparts than *argenteus*; head prominently streaked in winter; bill and legs rather pale yellow; bill-spot rather pale orange-red; less black on wing-tip than *argenteus*; and probably more likely to occur in winter than in summer), or *michahellis/cachinnans* from southern Europe/southern Asia (on average larger than *argenteus*; darker grey upperparts than *argenteus*; head white throughout year; bill and legs brighter yellow or orange-yellow than *argentatus/'omissus'/argenteus*; bill-spot brighter red than *argenteus/argentatus*; extent of black on wing-tip much as on *argenteus*; and probably more likely to occur in summer and autumn than in winter). The occurrence in northwest Europe of *michahellis* and *cachinnans* is shown by a very few recoveries of individuals ringed as nestlings on the Mediterranean (thus *michahellis*) and Black Sea (thus *cachinnans*). Subspecific identification of individual Herring Gulls with yellow legs in Britain or northwest Europe will not always be possible, but the average differences outlined above between *'omissus'* and *michahellis/cachinnans* should enable the majority to be assigned as 'showing the characters of' one or other subspecies. There are apparently only a very few recorded cases of *adult argenteus* with yellow (actually pale yellow) legs.

Subspecific identification of Herring Gulls requires careful observation at fairly close range, with good light (preferably not full sunlight) from behind the observer (so that colour tones can be correctly judged), and careful assessment of all of the important characters: size, bare-parts colour, extent of winter head-streaking, upper parts colour, and wing-tip pattern. It should be noted that the apparent shade of grey can change as a bird alters the angle of its body in relation to the observer. Obviously, it helps comparison if more than one subspecies is present.

The subspecific characters described above are largely based on museum skins, and their value in the field has in many cases not been tested. There is undoubtedly a lot more to be learned about the field characters of subspecies of Herring Gulls, and it is hoped that these summaries will encourage further attention by giving a broad base-line from which to work. Analysis of ringing recoveries could throw more light on the incompletely known winter distributions of the various subspecies.

Several authors have recommended specific status for the southern '*cachinnans*' group (thus Yellow-legged Gull *L. cachinnans*): this opinion is strengthened by the separate breeding behaviour of *michahellis* and *argenteus* in the same colony on Ile d'Oléron in the Bay of Biscay in 1976 (Nicolau-Guillaumet 1977). After range expansions south (*argenteus*) and north (*michahellis*) in recent years, this is the first meeting (at least in the western Palearctic) of the northern and southern subspecific groups of Herring Gulls.

Lesser Black-backed Gull
Larus fuscus

(Figs. 23c and 29, Photographs 200–217)

Adult summer

The identification summary, detailed descriptions and Figs. 23c and 29 refer to the west European race *L. f. graellsii*. Geographical variation is discussed on pages 92–93.

IDENTIFICATION

Lesser Black-backed Gull is slightly smaller than the west European race of Herring Gull *L. a. argenteus*, but with lighter general build and proportionately longer legs: the wings are proportionately longer, giving a slimmer-winged appearance in flight and a noticeably more attenuated rear end when perched. It is on average 20–30% smaller than Great Black-backed Gull, with proportionately much slimmer bill and smaller head, and proportionately longer wings and legs: it is generally much less bulky, and more attenuated at the rear end when perched. The size difference is very obvious when the two species are together.

The appearance of juveniles, and the differences from the similar juveniles of Herring and Great Black-backed Gulls, are described in Table 4 (pp. 80–81), and those of first-winter and first-summer plumages in the detailed descriptions.

In second-winter and second-summer plumages, the dark ash-grey begins to show on at least the mantle and scapulars, so there is little risk of confusion with Herring Gull. At these ages, it is best told from Great Black-backed by the generally darker and more extensive head markings, especially in winter when Great Black-backed is rather white-headed; generally darker underwing; and in summer by the dark

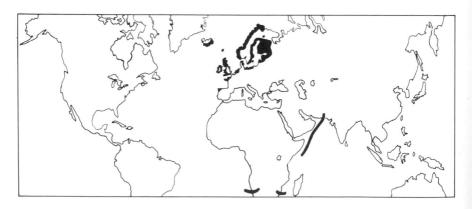

Fig. 28. World distribution of **Lesser Black-backed Gull** *Larus fuscus*, showing approximate breeding range (solid black) and approximate southern limit of winter/non-breeding range (black line). Now of regular occurrence in very small numbers in eastern coastal North America.

ash-grey rather than blackish upperparts (*L. f. graellsii* only). The size and structural differences, however, are perhaps the most reliable features at these ages.

Third-years and adults typically have extensive dark grey streaking or clouding on the head in winter (Great Black-backed has little, if any, dark streaking and remains generally white-headed in winter); dark ash-grey rather than blackish upperparts, contrasting with the black wing-tips (*L. f. graellsii* only); thinner tertial-crescent and smaller white tips to the primaries in fresh plumage, visible when perched (larger and prominent on Great Black-backed); one or two *small* white mirrors, (much more white on wing-tip on Great Black-backed); and yellowish or bright yellow legs (always flesh or creamy-flesh on Great Black-backed). A useful distinction of adults flying overhead is that the blackish primaries and secondaries form a complete dark trailing edge to the otherwise white underwing, whereas on adult Herring Gull only the outer primaries are dark.

First-year individuals (and to some extent, second-years), are relatively scarce in northern Europe; presumably the majority remains in the wintering/non-breeding areas during the first years of immaturity, and does not move north with the adults.

AGEING SUMMARY (see general discussion on ageing large gulls on pp. 69–70)

Juvenile: whole plumage fresh and unworn. Head and underparts rather uniformly streaked dark grey-brown. Neat scaly pattern on mantle and scapulars, uniformly barred wing-coverts. Bill black (summer to October).

First-winter: as juvenile, except dark patch on ear-coverts and scaly pattern on mantle and scapulars less well-defined (August to March).

First-summer: as first-winter, except head and underparts generally whiter; mantle, scapulars and upperwing more uniform and browner through fading, especially on coverts of inner wing (March to September).

Second-winter: extensive dusky head markings, variable amount of dark ash-grey on mantle and scapulars, and coverts of inner wing brownish, not neatly barred as on first-winter. Outer wing and secondary bar blackish, tail whiter than first-year with smaller subterminal band. Bill often extensively pale at base (September to March).

Second-summer: as second-winter, except head mainly white, mantle and scapulars mainly dark ash-grey, wings and tail becoming much worn and faded, and bill often yellowish at base (March to September).

Third-winter: as adult winter, except black wing-tip less clear cut and often lacking mirror, much brown freckling on inner wing, faint tail band, black subterminal band on bill (September to April).

Third-summer: as third-winter, except head white, wings faded to patchy brown and grey (not uniform as adult summer), and white primary tips reduced or lacking through wear (February to September).

Adult winter/fourth-winter: extensive dusky head markings, uniform dark ash-grey upperparts and wings, clear-cut black wing-tip with one or two mirrors, white tips to primaries obvious when perched, tail white, no black on bill (August to March).

Adult summer/fourth-summer: as adult winter, except head white, and white primary tips reduced or lacking through wear (February to September).

DETAILED DESCRIPTIONS

Juvenile See Table 4 (pp. 80–81)

First-winter (Figs. 23c and 29B, wings and tail similar to juvenile, 29A) Acquired by post-juvenile head and body moult, summer to November.

Appearance and identification as for juvenile, except ear-patch sometimes less prominent and scaly pattern on mantle and scapulars less well-defined. Upperparts generally darker and more uniform than first-winter Herring and Great Black-backed. Head and underparts often becoming whiter.

First-summer (Fig. 29C, underwing and tail similar to first-winter, 29B) Acquired by head and body moult, January to April.

Appearance and identification as for juvenile, except head and underparts generally whiter, wings and tail worn and faded, coverts (especially median and inner greater coverts) worn and often faded to pale brown, and mantle and scapulars less scaly, giving much more uniform brownish appearance than juvenile and first-winter, but retaining much darker general coloration than first summer Herring and Great Black-backed. Bill usually acquires pale base. Legs sometimes yellowish-flesh.

Second-winter (not illustrated, but wings and tail similar to second-summer, Fig. 29D) Acquired by complete moult, May to October.

HEAD White with extensive dusky streaking, usually concentrated around eye and on crown and lower hindneck.

BODY Underparts white, with extensive dark streaking and blackish mottling on breast-sides and flanks. Rump mainly white. Mantle and scapulars usually with much dark grey developing.

WINGS Outer wing and secondaries blackish. Inner wing-coverts mainly brown, with diffuse paler fringes. Underwing generally dark.

TAIL Mainly white, with prominent blackish subterminal band, less broad than on first-years.

BARE PARTS Iris sometimes becoming pale. Bill usually extensively pale with blackish subterminal area, but pattern highly variable. Legs flesh or yellowish-flesh.

Second-summer (Fig. 29D) Acquired by head and body moult, January to April.

As second-winter, except head and underparts generally whiter. Mantle and scapulars usually clear dark ash-grey, sometimes with a few brown-barred feathers. Blackish areas on wings and tail faded browner, and brown areas often faded to pale brown. Iris usually obviously pale. Bill often yellowish, with subterminal dark area of variable extent.

Third-winter (Fig. 29E) Acquired by complete moult, June to October.

HEAD White, with extensive dusky streaking or clouding, usually concentrated around eye and on crown and lower hindneck.

BODY Underparts mainly white, with variable amount of dark streaking. Rump white. Mantle and scapulars uniform dark ash-grey.

WINGS As adult winter, except black on outer wing less clear-cut and more

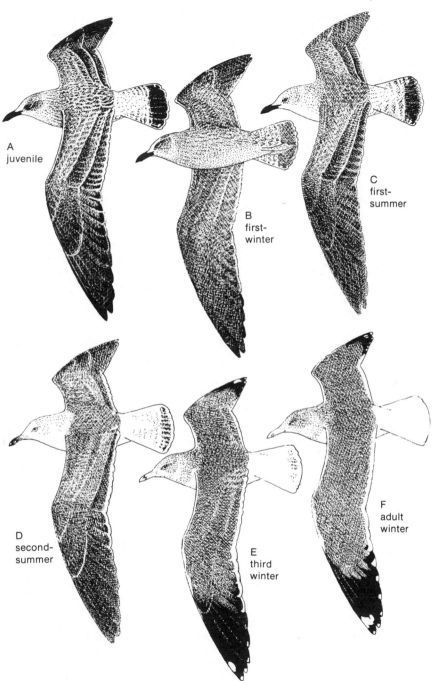

Fig. 29. **Lesser Black-backed Gulls** *Larus fuscus graellsii* in flight.

extensive, white primary tips usually smaller or lacking, and only one mirror, often none; extensive brown freckling on inner wing, especially on inner greater coverts and tertials, wing thus lacking general smart, uniform appearance of adult.

TAIL White, with usually faint subterminal band of varying extent and pattern.

BARE PARTS As adult, or bill with usually small dark subterminal mark or band, and legs yellowish-flesh, flesh, or greyish-flesh.

Third-summer (not illustrated, but wings and tail similar to third-winter, Fig. 29E) Acquired by head and body moult, January to April.

As third-winter, except head and underparts usually white, upperwing faded, patchy brown, especially on median and greater coverts and tertials; white primary tips reduced or lacking through wear.

Adult winter/fourth-winter (Fig. 29F) Acquired by complete moult, June to October.

HEAD AND BODY As third-winter.

WINGS Uniform dark ash-grey; scapular-crescent small, sometimes lacking; tertial-crescent prominent, obvious when perched, but on average less extensive and thinner than on Great Black-backed. Thin white leading edge, white tips to secondaries and inner primaries, forming prominent trailing edge. Black on outer primaries decreasing in extent inwards, usually to small subterminal spot on 7th, forming clear-cut black wing-tip. Outer primaries with neat white tips, smaller than on Great Black-backed, visible only when perched. Small mirror on outer primary (occasionally large and merging with white primary tip) and sometimes another (much smaller) on 2nd. Underwing white, with broad, dark grey subterminal trailing edge, merging with blackish undersides of outer primaries.

TAIL White.

BARE PARTS Iris pale yellow. Orbital ring red. Bill deep yellow, with red or orange-red spot near gonys and whitish tip (colours brighter than on Great Black-backed): some (possibly mainly fourth-winters) have blackish of variable extent on bill. Legs deep- or creamy-yellow: a few (as high as 3% in some large samples) have adult plumage but fleshy or greyish legs. These birds usually also have dark on the bill of variable extent, and are possibly fourth-winters which have yet to acquire fully adult bare parts coloration.

Adult summer/fourth summer (not illustrated, but wings and tail similar to adult winter, Fig. 29F) Acquired by head and body moult, January to May.

As adult winter, except head and underparts white, grey of upperparts and wings acquiring brownish tone through fading, white primary tips reduced or lacking through wear, and bill and legs generally bright orange-yellow.

GEOGRAPHICAL VARIATION

Barth (1975), in a detailed and convincing review of the taxonomy of Lesser Black-backed Gull, recognised three subspecies, distinguishable in the field mainly by the tone of grey on the upperparts of adults.

L. f. fuscus: Baltic area and northern Norway. Migrates mainly southeastwards, and is apparently the only subspecies wintering in the Middle East and east Africa.

Identification and ageing as *graellsii*, except upperparts of adult as black or blacker than Great Black-backed Gull, showing hardly any contrast with black wing-tip, often with brownish cast, probably through fading. Photographs and field observations from east Africa indicate that this subspecies remains white-headed in winter (P. L. Britton and N. van Swelm *in litt.*), unlike adult *intermedius* and *graellsii*, which acquire usually prominent dusky head-streaking. Adults begin the complete autumn moult from August (some two months later than *intermedius* and *graellsii*), sometimes after arrival in the wintering areas.

L. f. intermedius: Southern Norway, west Sweden and Denmark. Migration and winter range as *graellsii*. Identification and ageing as *graellsii*, except upperparts of adult blackish, slightly paler than Great Black-backed Gull, contrasting with black wing-tip. Often shows brownish cast probably through fading. Timing of autumn moult of adults as for *graellsii*.

L. f. graellsii: Iceland, Faeroes, British Isles, Netherlands, Brittany and northwest Spain. Migrates mainly south or southwestwards to wintering areas in western Europe and west Africa. Identification, ageing and timing of moult are covered in the detailed descriptions. Upperparts of adult dull smoky grey or dark ash-grey, obviously much darker than Herring Gull *L. a. argentatus/argenteus* and lacking the blackish tones of both *fuscus* and *intermedius*, and showing obvious contrast with the black wing-tip.

There is a good deal of intergradation in upperparts colour (and occasionally subspecifically mixed pairs) in some breeding colonies in Scandinavia (between *fuscus* and *intermedius*) and western Europe (between *intermedius* and *graellsii*), and in west European and west African wintering populations, nowhere more obvious than in Britain, where a proportion of individuals apparently match *fuscus* in their blackness. While typical examples of the three subspecies are readily distinguishable in the field (especially the distinctively pale-backed *graellsii*), fairly close-range observation, with good light (preferably not full sunlight) from behind the observer, is usually necessary for a correct assessment of colour tones. It should be noted that the apparent shade of grey can vary as a bird alters the angle of its body relative to the observer. My own observations of wintering and migrant Lesser Black-backed Gulls in southeast England suggest that the vast majority of blackish-backed Scandinavian birds are within the colour range of *intermedius:* a minority show the blackness of typical *fuscus* as described by Barth (1975) or shown by colour photographs of *fuscus* wintering in east Africa. Confusingly, some of this minority also have dark head-streaking, which is not a feature of *fuscus* wintering in East Africa.

On geographical grounds, it seems possible that some *fuscus* from breeding areas in northern Norway or southern Sweden are likely to migrate southwestwards (rather than southeastwards as in the case for the main *fuscus* population) and these may be the areas of origin of the *fuscus*-type Lesser Black-backeds occurring in Britain. An analysis of ringing recoveries would throw light on this possibility.

Great Black-backed Gull
Larus marinus

(Figs. 23B and 31, Photographs 218–239)

IDENTIFICATION

Adult summer

Great Black-backed Gull is markedly larger than Herring and Lesser Black-backed Gulls. Compared with the latter, it has a proportionately stouter bill and larger head, and proportionately shorter wings and legs; it is generally much more bulky, and less attenuated at the rear end when perched. The size difference is obvious when the two species are together. In flight, it has broader and proportionately shorter wings, giving a heavier, more lumbering appearance.

The appearance of juveniles, and the differences from the similar juveniles of Herring and Lesser Black-backed Gulls, are described in Table 4 (pp. 80–81), and those of first-winter and first-summer plumages in the detailed descriptions.

The main differences between Great Black-backed and Lesser Black-backed in second-year and subsequent plumages are summarised under Lesser Black-backed on pages 88–89.

AGEING SUMMARY (see general discussion on ageing large gulls on pp. 69–70)

Juvenile: whole plumage fresh and unworn. Underparts uniformly streaked grey-brown, head generally whiter. Neat, coarsely chequered pattern on mantle, scapulars and all coverts of inner wing: greater coverts with neat pattern of contrasting barring. Bill mainly black (summer to October).

First-winter: as juvenile, except head and body generally whiter, and mantle and scapulars less neatly chequered (August to March).

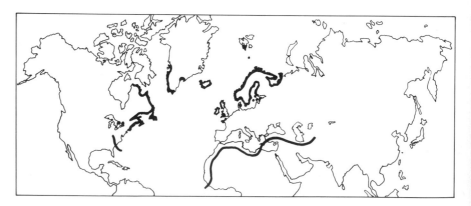

Fig. 30. World distribution of **Great Black-backed Gull** *Larus marinus*, showing approximate breeding range (solid black) and approximate southern limit of winter/non-breeding range (black line).

First-summer: as first-winter, except head and underparts whiter, mantle and scapulars more uniformly dark, but no clear blackish as on second-years (March to September).

Second-winter: mantle and scapulars with variable amount of clear blackish. Coverts of inner wing, especially greater coverts, generally more uniform grey-brown than on first-years. No clear-cut black and white on wing-tip. Extensive blackish on tail. Base of bill extensively pale (September to March).

Second-summer: as second-winter, except head and underparts mainly white, mantle and scapulars mainly uniform blackish. Bill often acquires some adult coloration (March to September).

Third-winter: as adult winter, except black on wing-tip less clear-cut and white less extensive; usually much brown freckling on inner wing. Faint tail band. Black subterminal mark or band on bill (September to April).

Third-summer: as third-winter, except wings faded patchy brown and black, and white primary tips reduced or lacking through wear (February to September).

Adult winter/fourth-winter: slight dusky head-streaking, uniform blackish upperparts and wings, extensive white on wing-tip, tail white, no black on bill (September to March).

Adult summer/fourth-summer: as adult winter, except head white, and white primary tips reduced or lacking through wear (February to September).

DETAILED DESCRIPTIONS

Juvenile See Table 4 (pp. 80–81).

First-winter (Figs. 23B and 31B, wings and tail similar to juvenile and first-summer, 31A and 31C) Acquired by post-juvenile head and body moult, summer to November.
Appearance and identification as for juvenile, except white-headed effect often more marked (although some dark streaking visible at close range, especially around eye and on lower hindneck). Mantle and scapulars less neatly chequered, but retaining general light and dark contrast. Bill sometimes paler at base, but not prominently pale-based as on Herring Gull.

First-summer (Fig. 31C, underwing and tail similar to first-winter, 31B) Acquired by head and body moult, January to April.
Appearance and identification as for juvenile, except head and underparts generally whiter, upperparts sometimes more uniformly dark with less contrasting chequered pattern, and bill often prominently tipped whitish and pale-based.

Second-winter (not illustrated, but similar to second-summer, Fig. 31D) Acquired by complete moult, May to October.
HEAD White, with faint dark streaking around eye and on lower hindneck.
BODY Underparts with extensive coarse dark streaking especially on breast-sides

and flanks. Rump mainly white. Mantle and scapulars usually with much clear dark grey or blackish, feathers otherwise whitish with brown bars.

WINGS Outer wing mainly blackish-brown, inner primaries slightly paler with blackish subterminal marks. Lesser and median coverts mainly rather uniform brownish; greater coverts rather uniform grey-brown: inner wings thus lacking strongly chequered or barred appearance of first-years. Secondary bar blackish. Underwing mainly dark, but coverts white, with dark markings. Outer primary sometimes with trace of mirror.

TAIL Whitish, with extensive blackish subterminal band.

BARE PARTS Iris sometimes becoming pale. Bill usually pale at base with extensive dark subterminal areas, but pattern highly variable. Legs as juvenile.

Second-summer (Fig. 31D) Acquired by head and body moult, January to April.

As second-winter, except head and underparts often white with few dark streaks. Mantle and scapulars mainly clear blackish, often with a few brown-barred feathers. Wings and tail worn and faded, coverts of inner wing acquiring general brownish appearance. Iris pale. Bill yellowish with subterminal dark area of variable extent.

Third-winter (Fig. 31E) Acquired by complete moult, June to November.

HEAD White, with dark eye-crescent and a few dark streaks mainly around eye and on lower hindneck: looks white-headed at long range.

BODY Underparts and rump white. Mantle and scapulars uniform blackish-grey.

WINGS As adult winter, except black more extensive and white primary tips and mirror on 2nd smaller; extensive brown freckling on inner wing, especially on inner greater coverts and tertials, thus wings lacking smart, uniform appearance of adult.

TAIL White, with usually faint subterminal band of variable extent and pattern.

BARE PARTS Bill usually whitish or fleshy-yellow, often with some reddish on gonys, with prominent, neat black subterminal band, but pattern highly variable.

Third-summer (not illustrated, but similar to third-winter, Fig. 31E) Acquired by head and body moult, January to April.

As third-winter, except head and underparts white, patchy appearance of upper-wing more pronounced, upperparts acquiring brownish tone due to fading, and white primary tips reduced through wear.

Adult winter/fourth-winter (Fig. 31F) Acquired by complete moult, June to January. In view of this species' larger size, it seems likely that a higher proportion do not acquire full adult plumage at this age than is the case with other large gulls, showing signs of immaturity especially on inner wing-coverts, tail and bill.

HEAD AND BODY As third-winter.

WINGS Uniform blackish-grey, looking black at long range; scapular-crescent small; tertial-crescent extensive and obvious when perched. Thin white leading edge; white tips to secondaries and inner primaries forming prominent trailing edge. Black on outer primaries decreasing in extent inwards, usually to subterminal mark on 6th, forming black wing-tip which, at close range, contrasts with the blackish-grey remainder. Outer primaries with large white tips, on 1st merging with large mirror to form extensive white end to feather: this, and the large mirror on 2nd form diagnostic wing-tip pattern. Underwing white, with broad, dark grey subterminal trailing edge which merges with blackish undersides of outer primaries.

TAIL White.

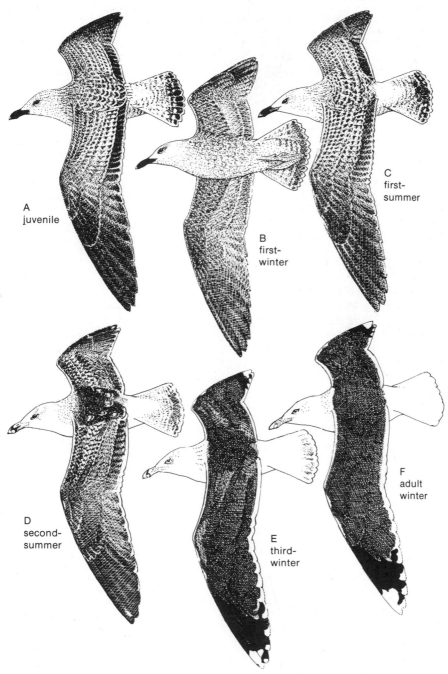

Fig. 31. **Great Black-backed Gulls** *Larus marinus* in flight.

BARE PARTS Iris pale yellow. Orbital ring red. Bill pale yellow or fleshy-yellow, with orange or red spot on gonys; colours generally paler than Lesser Black-backed. Legs flesh or creamy-flesh.

Adult summer/fourth-summer (not illustrated, but similar to adult winter, Fig. 31F) Acquired by head and body moult, January to May.

As adult winter, except head and body white, blackish-grey of upperparts and wings acquiring brownish tone through fading, white primary tips reduced through wear, and bare parts perhaps generally brighter.

Great Black-headed Gull
Larus ichthyaetus

(Figs. 23D and 33, Photographs 240–260)

IDENTIFICATION   *Adult summer*

Great Black-headed Gull is usually obviously larger than Herring Gull. When perched, it often matches Great Black-backed in length, but its build is not as heavy, the wings are proportionately longer and extend farther beyond the tail (giving a more attenuated rear end), and the legs are proportionately longer; the tertials are sometimes held loosely folded, projecting as a prominent 'hump' from the line of the lower back. The head shape is distinctive; the long, sloping forehead, which peaks well behind the eye, gives a heavy 'snout' effect, which accentuates the length and heaviness of the bill. In flight, the deep chest, long head and heavy bill may give a front-heavy impression; it has proportionately more pointed, slimmer and longer wings than other large gulls. These structural features are important at all ages.

Great Black-headed Gulls, especially immatures, could easily be overlooked when perched among other large gulls, but in flight have a very distinctive appearance at all ages.

The juvenile has a rather pale head and brown mantle and scapulars—the latter with pale fringes giving a prominent scaly pattern—and, unlike any other immature large gull, prominent brownish lower hindneck and breast-side patches (or complete breast-band) contrasting sharply with the clear white remainder of the underparts. Surprisingly in view of its large size, Great Black-headed normally acquires a mainly clear grey mantle and scapulars and white underparts in the first winter, a pattern more like that of some medium-sized gulls of the same age, and quite unlike the

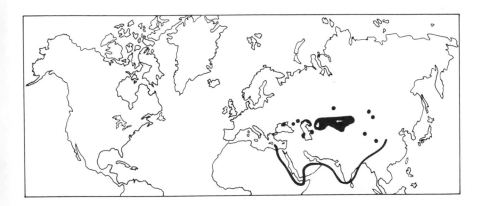

Fig. 32.   World distribution of **Great Black-headed Gull** *Larus ichthyaetus*, showing approximate breeding range (solid black) and approximate southern limit of regular winter/non-breeding range (black line). A rare vagrant to western Europe, with five records prior to 1932 and only one since.

extensively dark mantle and body of other first-winter large gulls. The head of first-winters is white, with dark markings behind the eye, usually forming a prominent dark patch, and dark streaking concentrated on the lower hindneck, often extending to dark breast-side patches. The outer greater coverts are mainly pale grey-brown, forming a uniform and striking pale midwing panel. The underwing is mainly white with an obvious, translucent window, and the tail is white, with a broad, clear-cut black subterminal band: patterns unlike any other first-year large gull. In first-summer plumage, a partial or full hood is sometimes acquired. Throughout the first year, the bill is pale, with clear-cut black tip or subterminal band.

In second-year plumages, the outer primaries and their coverts are mainly blackish, but the inner primaries and inner wing are mainly clear grey, usually with a few brown coverts and an indistinct secondary bar. The subterminal tail band is thinner than on first-years, and the bare parts usually begin to acquire some adult coloration. A partial or full hood is usually acquired in second-summer plumage.

Third-years closely resemble adults, but have more extensive black on the primaries and less white on the tips, and usually a faint tail band.

Adults are unmistakable: Great Black-headed is the only large gull with a black hood in summer, reduced to a dark mask behind the eye in winter. The wing pattern is diagnostic: the mantle and scapulars are rather dark grey (darker than on Black-headed Gull), shading to pale pearly-grey on the inner wing, with a very broad, rather well-defined white trailing edge, and the outer wing is mainly white, with a neat subterminal crescent of black across the outer primaries. At a distance in flight, the mantle and scapulars may appear rather dark grey, shading paler across the inner wing to mainly white secondaries and primaries: at very long range, the restricted black on the wing-tips of some adults may be difficult to discern. The bill is mainly yellow, with a prominent black subterminal band and reddish tip. The legs are greenish-yellow.

Large gulls with patches of oil on the head, or abnormal concentrations of the usual dark head-streaking in winter, may at times suggest this species, but examination at least of the wing and tail patterns will avoid the slight misidentification risk in such cases.

AGEING SUMMARY

Juvenile: pale head, brownish breast-side patches or broad breast-band, scaly brown upperparts (summer to October).

First-winter: winter head pattern, white underparts with brownish breast-side patches, mainly uniform pale grey mantle and scapulars. Blackish-brown outer primaries, secondary bar and broad tail band. Brownish wing-coverts, and pale grey-brown midwing panel (August to April).

First-summer: as first-winter, except sometimes hood of variable extent, wings and tail faded, and brownish carpal area reduced (February to September).

Second-winter: winter head pattern, upperparts and wings mainly uniform pale grey, outer primaries and coverts mainly black, clear-cut, thin black tail band (July to April).

Second-summer: as second-winter, except usually with partial or full hood (February to September).

Third-winter: as adult winter, except outer primaries with more black and less white at tips. Usually a faint tail band (July to April).

Third-summer: as third winter, but hood fully developed (January to September).

Adult winter/fourth-winter: winter head pattern, outer wing mainly white with subterminal crescent of black across outer primaries and extensive white at tips. Tail white (August to February).

Adult summer/fourth-summer: as adult winter, full black hood (January to September).

DETAILED DESCRIPTIONS

Juvenile (Fig. 33A, underwing and tail similar to first winter, 33B).
HEAD White (sometimes with variable amount of brown streaking behind eye), contrasting with darker hindneck and breast-sides. Thin white crescents above and below eye; eye crescent dusky.
BODY Underparts white, with brownish mottling on breast-sides, often joining in centre to form fairly clear-cut breast-band, sometimes extending onto flanks. Rump and vent mainly white, usually with a few dark spots on upper- and undertail coverts. Mantle and scapulars rich brown, with pale feather fringes forming strong scaly pattern.
WINGS Carpal-bar brown, with pale feather fringes. Outer greater coverts uniform pale greyish or brownish-grey, with dark centres; inner greater coverts and tertials brown, with clear-cut pale fringes. Secondaries blackish, with white fringes, and white on inner webs increasing in extent inwards. Outer wing mainly blackish-brown, inner three or four primaries sometimes with broad, clear-cut pale margins: white on inner webs of primaries increasing in extent inwards from 2nd or 3rd. Underwing-coverts white, with sparse dark markings in lines.
TAIL White, with broad, clear-cut blackish subterminal band, width about one-third of tail length, usually extending to outer web of outer feather, which is, however, often fringed with or wholly white.
BARE PARTS Iris dark. Orbital ring dark grey. Bill greyish or flesh basally, with extensive diffuse black tip. Legs lead grey, brownish-grey or flesh.

First-winter (Figs. 23D and 33B, wing and tail pattern similar to first-summer, 33C) Acquired by post-juvenile head and body moult, summer to September. *As juvenile, except:*
HEAD AND BODY White, with dusky markings around eye often faint or almost lacking, but typically forming a defined patch from behind eye, extending diffusely over crown. Prominent white crescent above and below eye. Hindneck streaked or neatly spotted with blackish-brown, concentrated in a dense patch on lower hindneck (contrasting sharply with grey mantle), often extending prominently onto breast-sides. Mantle and scapulars clear pale grey, or with a few brown feathers, but sometimes mainly brown.

WINGS Dark areas becoming faded and browner, especially inner primaries and their coverts which form a prominent pale window.

TAIL White tips and fringes often lacking through wear.

BARE PARTS Base of bill paler, sometimes yellowish, with clear-cut black tip or broad subterminal band.

First-summer (Fig. 33c, underwing and tail similar to first-winter, 33b) Acquired by head and body moult, January to April. *As first-winter, except:*

HEAD Black usually more extensive; a few may acquire partial or full hood and lose the dark hindneck.

WINGS AND TAIL Becoming much worn and faded, mid-wing panel often whitish.

BARE PARTS As first-winter, or bill yellowish with clear-cut subterminal band, and legs with greenish tone.

Second-winter (not illustrated, but wing and tail pattern similar to second-summer, Fig. 33d) Acquired by complete moult, April to October.

HEAD White, with dusky markings forming well-defined patch from behind eye, often extending diffusely over crown. Hindneck streaked or spotted blackish, concentrated in patch on lower hindneck.

BODY Underparts and rump white. Upperparts uniform grey, perhaps slightly darker and browner in tone than on adult. Thin white scapular- and prominent tertial-crescent. Inner wing with faint secondary bar and usually a few brown coverts; outer primaries and their coverts with extensive blackish, decreasing in extent inwards to small subterminal marks on 7th to 9th: outer wing thus with much black along leading edge. Underwing white, except for black on outer primaries and a few dusky marks on coverts.

TAIL White with prominent subterminal black band, thinner than first-year.

BARE PARTS Bill yellowish with clear-cut black subterminal band and pale tip. Legs dusky, greenish or yellowish.

Second-summer (Fig. 33d) Acquired by head and body moult, January to April.

As second-winter, except partial or full hood usually acquired, white primary tips and terminal tail fringe reduced or lacking through wear, bill sometimes more orange-yellow, and legs usually yellowish.

Third-winter (Fig. 33e) Acquired by complete moult, May to October. Some probably become indistinguishable from adults at this age. *As adult winter, except:*

WINGS Black on outer primaries more extensive and less white at tips; wing-tip looks wholly black at long range.

TAIL Faint or spotted tail band usually present.

Third-summer (not illustrated, but wings and tail as third-winter, Fig. 33e) Acquired by head and body moult, January to April.

As third-winter, except full hood usually acquired, and white primary tips reduced or lacking through wear.

Adult winter/fourth-winter (not illustrated, but wings and tail similar to adult summer, Fig. 33f) Acquired by complete moult, May to November.

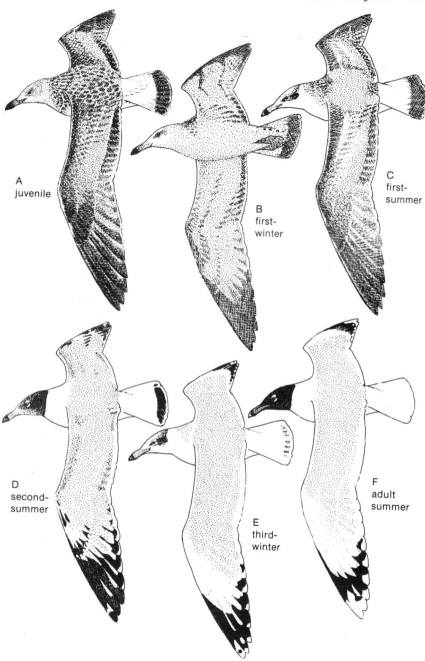

Fig. 33. **Great Black-headed Gulls** *Larus ichthyaetus* in flight.

HEAD AND BODY As second-winter, except upperparts grey, with thin whitish fringes to most scapulars, giving delicate scaly pattern.

WINGS Inner wing and inner primaries pale pearly-grey, with thin white leading edge and broad white trailing edge. Outer primary with complete black outer web, extensive subterminal black and large white tip; subterminal black decreasing inwards usually to a small spot on 6th, but precise pattern of black and white highly variable. Remainder of outer wing white, forming a prominent triangle of white along the leading edge; often the whole of the outer wing looks white, apart from the subterminal crescent of black across the outer primaries. Underwing white, with faint grey bar across greater underwing coverts.

TAIL White.

BARE PARTS As second-winter.

Adult summer/fourth-summer (Fig. 33F) Acquired by head and body moult, January to April. *As adult winter, except:*

HEAD White, with extensive black hood. Thick white crescents or oval patches posteriorly above and below eye.

WINGS White primary tips reduced through wear.

BARE PARTS Iris dark brown. Orbital ring red. Bill yellow or orange-yellow, with neat black subterminal band and reddish or orange-red tip. Mouth and gape dull red. Legs yellow or greenish-yellow.

Little, Ross's, Sabine's and Ivory Gulls and Kittiwake

The species in this group, except Ivory Gull *Pagophila eburnea*, are small- to medium-sized gulls which share, in their first year, a striking W pattern across the wings in flight (unlike any other western Palearctic gull), causing possible confusion especially at long range. Adults have a more distinctive appearance, making confusion less likely. Ivory Gull is the largest of this group (slightly larger than Common Gull *Larus canus*), and is unmistakable at all ages—white with sparse black spots in its first year, and all-white when adult.

Sabine's Gull *L. sabini* has a complete moult in spring, and a head and body moult in autumn, the reverse of the moult timing of other gulls: a complete early spring moult from first-winter takes place in winter quarters, and in the resultant first-summer plumage most resemble adults except for an incomplete hood. Ross's Gull *Rhodostethia rosea*, Ivory Gull and most Kittiwakes *Rissa tridactyla* acquire adult plumage in their second winter. Little Gull *L. minutus* is exceptional in this group, in that probably the majority are readily ageable in second-year plumages.

Ross's, Sabine's and Ivory Gulls (Figs. 37, 39 and 43) are among the most sought-after and beautiful of Arctic rarities; only Sabine's regularly moves south of the Arctic seas, at least the major part—if not all—of the population being highly migratory, wintering in the southern oceans. Kittiwake (Fig. 41) is an almost exclusively marine and coastal gull, familiar in most of the northern hemisphere. Little Gull (Fig. 35) typically frequents marshes, inland lakes, and sheltered coasts; on migration and in favoured breeding and wintering areas it may be locally

Table 5: Measurements (mm) of five gulls (from Dwight 1925)

	sample	wing	tail	bill	tarsus
Little Gull *Larus minutus*	25	210–230	85–97	21–25	25–29
Ross's Gull *Rhodostethia rosea*	11	248–265	121–138	18–20	30–33
Sabine's Gull *Larus sabini*	25	245–284	108–131	22–28	31–38
Ivory Gull *Pagophila eburnea*	20	320–346	135–160	32–38	35–42
Kittiwake *Rissa tridactyla*	22	285–322	113–140	31–40	31–36

numerous, but in most of its range it is perhaps the least familiar of the commoner gulls. Familiarity with immature Little Gulls and Kittiwakes will greatly aid recognition of Ross's and Sabine's Gulls respectively.

Fig. 34.　First-winter **Little** *Larus minutus*, **Ross's** *Rhodostethia rosea* and **Ivory Gulls** *Pagophila eburnea*, and **Kittiwake** *Rissa tridactyla*, and juvenile **Sabine's Gull** *L. sabini*, showing comparative sizes, shapes and stances.

Little Gull

Larus minutus

(Figs. 35A and 36, Photographs 261–275)

Second-winter

IDENTIFICATION

Little Gull is the smallest of the world's gulls, with a wing span 20–30% less than that of Black-headed Gull *L. ridibundus* or Kittiwake. On second-years and adults the wing-tip is slightly more rounded than on other similar gulls, and this shape is further accentuated by the even more rounded pattern of the subterminal grey (above) and blackish (below) on the outer primaries. On first-years the wing-tip is not appreciably more rounded than on other gulls. The tail is square-ended or (on some first-years) very slightly forked. It is a dainty, non-scavenging species, which usually feeds by picking from the water surface in flight.

In first-year plumages, the combination of small size and striking W pattern across the wings in flight makes identification straightforward. Of the regular western Palearctic gulls, only first-year Kittiwake (p. 121) has a similar pattern, and in situations where the size difference is not immediately apparent, the best distinctions are juvenile Little Gulls' mainly dark brown mantle, scapulars and back (upperparts grey on juvenile Kittiwake), blackish cap, flesh-coloured or reddish legs (usually black on Kittiwake), indistinct, dark secondary bar (Kittiwake has all-white secondaries), and inner greater primary coverts mainly blackish (wholly grey on Kittiwake). Juvenile and some first-winter Kittiwakes have a diagnostic clear-cut, black half-collar on the lower hindneck, but note that a similar mark is shown by autumn Little Gulls which are in a transitional stage of moult from juvenile to first-winter plumage (but these individuals will always also retain the blackish-brown patch on the back, never

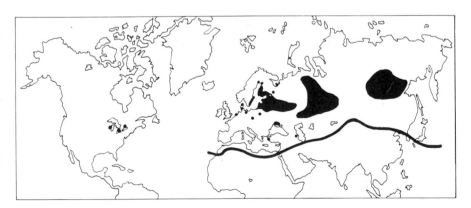

Fig. 35. World distribution of **Little Gull** *Larus minutus*, showing approximate breeding range (solid black) and approximate southern limit of winter/non-breeding range (black line). Since the first in 1962, there have been several breeding records in the Great Lakes area, together with a general increase in sight records in eastern North America.

shown by Kittiwake). Little Gulls moulting from first-summer to second-winter show a strikingly patchy transitional underwing pattern caused by the contrast between the new blackish coverts and inner primaries and the old white first-year feathers. First-year Bonaparte's *L. philadelphia* (p. 32 and Ross's Gulls (p. 112), both vagrants to Europe, also resemble first-year Little Gull and are only slightly larger: the differences are described in the respective species accounts.

Given good views of the wing pattern, probably the majority of second-year Little Gulls are readily ageable: they resemble adults except for black subterminal marks of very variable pattern on the upperside of the outer primaries and the lack of a uniformly blackish underwing. Note, however, that a second-year upperwing pattern can be suggested in autumn by adults in a transitional stage of moult from summer to winter plumage, retaining old, worn outer primaries which look darker than the fresh inner ones.

In second-year and adult plumages, Little Gull is unlikely to be confused with any other species; even at long range, the alternation, with each wingbeat, of blackish underwing and pale grey upperwing is distinctive. In summer at least, the underparts are invariably obviously pink-flushed, unlike other common species.

AGEING SUMMARY

Juvenile: as first-winter, but extensive blackish-brown on mantle and scapulars extending to breast-sides (summer to October).

First-winter: uniform grey mantle and scapulars, bold blackish W pattern across wings in flight, black tail band, winter head pattern (August to April).

First-summer: as first-winter, but W pattern faded, tail band often broken in centre, hood usually developed to variable extent (March to October).

Second-winter: as adult winter, but underwing-coverts paler or whitish, and variable pattern of black subterminal marks on upperside of wing-tip (August to April).

Second-summer: as second-winter, but hood usually fully developed (March to October).

Adult winter/third-winter: upperwing grey with white border on trailing edge and tip, underwing uniformly blackish, tail white, winter head pattern (August to April).

Adult summer/third-summer: as adult winter, but with full black hood (February to October).

DETAILED DESCRIPTIONS

Juvenile (Fig. 36A. Underwing and tail similar to first-winter, 36C)
HEAD White, with blackish-brown eye-crescent, ear-spot, crown and hindneck.
BODY Mantle, back and scapulars blackish-brown, with whitish fringes giving scaly pattern most prominent on scapulars. Underparts and rump white, except for blackish-brown patches on breast-sides (extension of mantle colour).
WINGS Coverts of inner wing pale grey, except for clear-cut, broad, blackish-

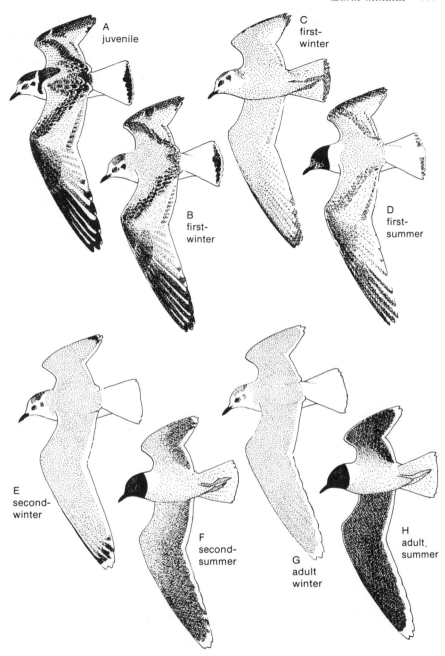

Fig. 36. **Little Gulls** *Larus minutus* in flight.

brown carpal-bar: tertials and inner greater and median coverts with neat whitish fringes. Apparently very rare variant has upperwing-coverts almost wholly blackish-brown. Secondaries pale grey, with broad white tips and blackish centres, latter forming broken, dark subterminal bar on trailing edge of inner wing. Alula and outer coverts of outer wing mainly blackish, innermost coverts mainly pale grey. Black on outer web and tip of outer primaries decreasing in extent inwards to small subterminal spot on 6th or 7th (rarely 8th); white tips to primaries increasing in size inwards from 2nd or 3rd. Inner primaries grey on outer webs, broadly tipped white. Inner webs of all primaries mainly white. Underwing white, except for exposed blackish tips of outer primaries and black leading edge of 1st.

TAIL White, with clear-cut, black band (and narrow, whitish terminal fringe) broadest in centre (accentuating the slightly forked tail-shape of some individuals); sometimes outer pair of feathers, rarely two outer pairs, all-white.

BARE PARTS Iris and orbital ring blackish. Bill blackish; mouth flesh. Legs pale flesh or reddish.

First-winter (Figs. 34A, 36B and 36C) Acquired by post-juvenile head and body moult which starts at fledging and is usually complete by November. *As juvenile, except:*

HEAD White, with dark grey or blackish eye-crescent, ear-spot and crown; hindneck grey (extension of mantle colour).

BODY Mantle, back and scapulars pale grey, often with a few retained juvenile feathers on back and scapulars. Breast-sides grey (extension of mantle colour).

WINGS AND TAIL White terminal spots on primaries, and terminal fringe on tail, reduced or lacking through wear.

First-summer (Fig. 36D depicts a particularly worn and faded individual in late summer. Underwing and tail similar to first-winter, 36C) Acquired by moult of head, body, and usually one or more pairs of central tail feathers and some inner wing-coverts, February to May. *As first-winter, except:*

HEAD Partial or full hood of grey, brown or black sometimes acquired, and grey on hindneck lost.

BODY Some acquire pink flush on underparts and lose grey breast-sides.

WINGS Becoming much worn and faded by late summer, and dark areas, especially carpal-bar (which is often less extensive), often fade to pale brown.

TAIL Band often faded to pale brown and white terminal fringe lacking through wear; tail band often broken in centre by one or more pairs of newly-grown, all-white feathers. Tail rarely wholly white.

BARE PARTS Legs and mouth dull red.

Individuals in transition from first-summer to second-winter plumage in autumn have strikingly patchy blackish and white underwing patterns.

Second-winter (Fig. 36E. Underwing and tail similar to second-summer, 36F) Acquired by complete moult, June to October. *As adult winter, except:*

WINGS Outer webs of two to six outer primaries with subterminal or terminal blackish marks of variable extent and pattern. Sometimes, outer greater primary coverts, alula, inner secondaries and tertials have small blackish-brown marks which are occasionally extensive. Axillaries white; median and lesser underwing coverts whitish or grey, contrasting with grey or blackish remainder of underwing (underwing thus never uniformly blackish as on adult).

An unknown proportion probably become indistinguishable from adults at this age. Blackish subterminal marks on the outer primaries are a certain indication of second-year, and individuals with these marks invariably also have obviously pale underwing-coverts. Individuals with adult-type upperwing pattern and obviously pale underwing-coverts are probably second-years. The black marks on the wing-tip are most easily visible on the closed wing when perched, but should not be confused with the black underside of the outer primaries shown by perched adults.

Second-summer (Fig. 36F. Upperwing and tail similar to second-winter, 36E) Acquired by head and body moult, February to May.

As adult summer, except upper- and underwing as second-winter, although white border and dark marks on wing-tip reduced through wear. Hood usually fully developed or white-flecked, but a few have winter head pattern. Legs dull red.

Adult winter/third-winter (Fig. 36G. Underwing and tail as adult summer, 36H) Acquired by complete moult, June to November.

HEAD White, with blackish eye-crescent and ear-spot, and grey crown and hindneck.

BODY Mantle, back and scapulars uniform pale grey with white scapular-crescent faint or lacking. Breast-sides grey (extension of mantle colour), rump and remainder of underparts white; underparts sometimes flushed pink.

WINGS Upperwing uniformly pale grey, all primaries and secondaries broadly tipped white, forming prominent white border on trailing edge and tip of wing. Axillaries pale grey, median and lesser underwing-coverts dark grey, remainder of underwing blackish with white border on trailing edge and tip.

TAIL White, square-ended.

BARE PARTS Iris and orbital ring blackish brown. Bill blackish; mouth red or orange-red. Legs dull red.

Adult summer/third-summer (Fig. 36H. Upperwing and tail as adult winter, 36G) Acquired by head and body moult, January to May.

As adult winter, except black hood extending over whole head and upper neck. Whole underparts and hindneck flushed with pink, especially obvious on breast. Bill dark reddish-brown. Legs scarlet.

Ross's Gull
Rhodostethia rosea

(Figs. 35ʙ and 38, Photographs 276–287)

Adult summer

IDENTIFICATION

This beautiful small gull of the High Arctic resembles Little Gull in some plumages, and could be overlooked as such at long range. In body size, it is only slightly—if at all—larger than Little Gull, but the wings and tail are proportionately much longer, giving a strikingly attenuated rear end when swimming or on the ground. In flight, the wing-tips are pointed (not slightly rounded as on Little Gull), and the end of the tail is diagnostically wedge-shaped (although this may be difficult to discern at long range), with the central pair of feathers more elongated and projecting farther than the rest. When feeding it has a leisurely, buoyant flight, with noticeably long wings, hovering to take food from the surface or dropping momentarily onto the water, or sometimes plunge-diving like a Kittiwake. It also feeds when swimming, picking at the surface in the manner of a phalarope *Phalaropus*. In direct flight, it has rather pigeon-like, fast, deep wing-beats. On the ground, it is strikingly reminiscent of a dove *Streptopelia*, a compound effect of its small bill, rather small, domed head, full chest, short legs, feathered thighs and, especially, its short-stepping, head-nodding gait.

In first-year plumages, it has a striking W pattern across the wings in flight, but the black on the outer primaries is less extensive than on Little Gull, and the secondaries are clear white without a dark bar, forming a broad white trailing edge to the inner wing which extends across the outer wing almost to the outer edge near the wing-tip.

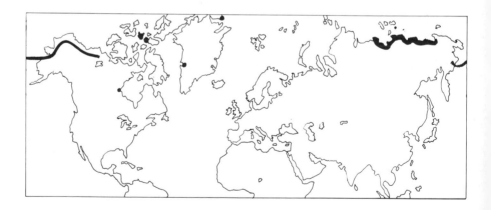

Fig. 37.   World distribution of **Ross's Gull** *Rhodostethia rosea*, showing approximate regular breeding range (solid black), and approximate sites of recent proved breeding in Greenland, Canadian Arctic and Manitoba. Approximate southern limit of winter/non-breeding range of Siberian population is shown by black line. Rare south of Arctic seas, in Britain and Ireland averaging about one record annually.

The black on the tail is more confined to the centre, not forming an almost complete band as on Little Gull. In first-summer plumage, the wing-pattern may become much faded, and some acquire an adult-type neck-ring.

Probably the majority acquire adult plumage in their second winter. Occasionally, however, individuals in otherwise adult plumage show such immature characters as traces of a carpal-bar, dark marks near the tips of the outer two or more primaries, or dusky marks on the innermost secondaries, and such birds can be safely aged as second-years; individuals which retain winter-type head and body plumage in summer may be in second-summer plumage.

Adults in winter differ from Little Gull in lacking a prominent dark cap, the underwing is grey, not blackish, and the upperwing has a broad, white trailing edge confined to the secondaries and inner primaries, not a complete, relatively thin border as on Little Gull. The underparts are often obviously pink-flushed even in winter. Summer adults are unmistakable, with diagnostic black neck-ring and, usually, intensely pink underparts, this colour being most obvious in overcast condition.

An identification pitfall is provided by immature and adult Little Gulls in autumn, which, at a transitional stage of moult, may have a wedge-shaped tail (caused by outer tail feathers which are not fully grown) and unfamiliar plumage patterns. In some lighting at long range, the black of the centrally-broken tail band on some first-summer Little Gulls may not be discernible, so that the tail appears to be all-white and wedge-shaped.

AGEING SUMMARY

Juvenile: as first-winter, but extensive blackish-brown on mantle and scapulars, extending to breast-sides (summer to October).

First-winter: uniform grey mantle and scapulars, bold blackish W pattern across wings in flight, black bar on tail, winter head pattern (August to April).

First-summer: as first-winter, but W pattern faded; some acquire partial or complete neck-ring and/or pink flush on underparts (March to September).

Adult winter/second-winter: upperwing grey with broad white trailing edge to inner wing, tail white, winter head pattern, underparts often pink-flushed (August to April).

Adult summer/second-summer: as adult winter, but with full neck-ring and usually intensely pink underparts (February to October).

DETAILED DESCRIPTIONS

Juvenile (Fig. 38A)
HEAD White, with blackish-brown eye-crescent, ear-spot, crown and hindneck.
BODY Mantle, back, upper rump and scapulars blackish-brown, with buff or golden fringes, giving scaly effect most prominent on scapulars. Underparts and lower rump white, except for blackish-brown patches on breast-sides (extension of mantle colour).
WINGS Coverts of inner wing pale grey, except for clear-cut, blackish-brown carpal-bar (individual feathers fringed whitish) and mainly very pale grey or whitish

greater coverts. Innermost secondaries with small black marks, remainder white. Alula and coverts of outer wing mainly blackish, innermost coverts grey. Outer web and half of inner web of outer three primaries black, except sometimes for small white area on outer web near tip of 3rd and occasionally also 2nd. Blackish on base of outer web of 4th decreasing in extent inwards to 6th or 7th; black on tips decreasing in extent inwards from 4th to small black subterminal marks on 7th or 8th; remainder of 4th to 10th whitish. Marginal coverts of inner and outer wing white. Underwing-coverts washed grey, with broad translucent trailing edge to underwing on secondaries and inner primaries; outer web of 1st and exposed tips of outer primaries black.

TAIL Long uppertail-coverts finely tipped black. Tail markedly wedge-shaped, white with broad black subterminal area on elongated central pair (terminal fringe buff), black decreasing in extent outwards, usually to small terminal mark on 3rd outermost (two outer pairs usually all-white). Black on tail sometimes confined to only two central pairs of feathers. From below, black on tail often obscured by long, white undertail-coverts.

BARE PARTS Iris and orbital ring blackish. Bill blackish, sometimes with reddish-brown at base; mouth flesh. Legs brown, dull flesh or dull red.

First-winter (Figs. 34B and 38B) Acquired by head and body moult, summer to September. *As juvenile, except:*

HEAD White, with grey-washed crown and hindneck (extension of mantle colour) and blackish ear spot and eye-crescent, latter usually extensive in front of and below eye, often appearing as dark mask. Thin white crescents above and below eye.

BODY Mantle and scapulars uniform pale grey, sometimes with a few retained blackish juvenile feathers on scapulars and back; faint white scapular- and tertial-crescents. Breast-sides or whole upper breast and upper flanks washed grey (extension of mantle colour).

First-summer (Fig. 38C depicts a particularly faded individual in late summer) Acquired by head and body moult, February to May. *As first-winter, except:*

HEAD Partial or full neck-ring often acquired.

BODY Many acquire pink flush on underparts and/or lose grey on breast and flanks.

WINGS Becoming much worn by late summer, and dark areas, especially the carpal-bar, often fade to brownish.

TAIL Black faded and reduced through wear.

BARE PARTS Orbital ring sometimes reddish.

Second-winter and **second-summer**

Some second-year individuals may be aged, as described in identification section, page 112.

Adult winter/second-winter (Fig. 38D) Acquired by complete moult, June to September.

HEAD As first-winter, but eye-crescent and ear-spot sometimes very faint or lacking. Partial or full neck-ring sometimes retained.

BODY As first-winter, but without retained juvenile feathers. Underparts often obviously pink-flushed.

WINGS Upperwing uniform pale grey except for black outer web almost to tip of 1st primary, white tips to inner primaries increasing in extent inwards from 6th to

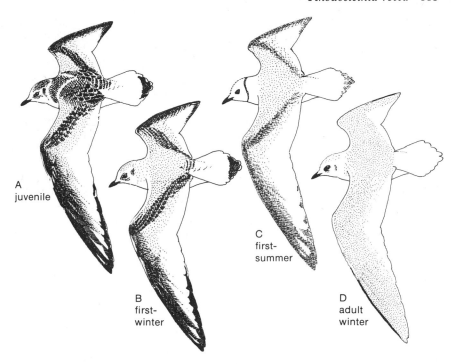

A
juvenile

B
first-
winter

C
first-
summer

D
adult
winter

Fig. 38. **Ross's Gulls** *Rhodostethia rosea* in flight.

almost all-white 10th, and all-white secondaries. Vestigial outermost primary occasionally black on outer web. Underwing-coverts and undersides of outer primaries pale grey of same tone or darker than upperwing, but often appearing much darker than upperwing in the field, through effect of shadow. Axillaries washed grey. White secondaries and tips of inner primaries form broad, translucent trailing edge. Marginal coverts of inner and outer wing white.

TAIL White.

BARE PARTS Much as juvenile, but legs sometimes red or reddish.

Adult summer/second-summer (not illustrated, but head as first-summer, Fig. 38C, and wing and tail pattern as adult winter, 38D) Acquired by head and body moult, February to May. *As adult winter, except:*

HEAD White, with neat black collar around nape and lower throat, thickest on nape and at rear of ear-coverts, and thinnest on throat, sometimes incomplete or lower portion concealed by feather overlap. Crown sometimes washed grey.

BODY Usually, whole underparts, sides of neck and hindneck pink of apparently varying strength, usually intense: this variation may be largely illusory, the pink being most obvious in overcast conditions. Rump white, sometimes washed pink.

WINGS and TAIL Becoming worn by late summer, especially elongated central tail feathers, which are frequently broken short.

BARE PARTS Iris blackish-brown, orbital ring red. Bill blackish, mouth red. Legs orange-red.

Sabine's Gull
Larus sabini

(Figs. 35c and 40, Photographs 288–299)

Juvenile

IDENTIFICATION

Away from the breeding grounds, Sabine's Gull is almost wholly pelagic. The Nearctic population migrates on a diagonal route across the north Atlantic to wintering areas off southwest Africa; the occasional sightings from west European coasts are usually the result of westerly gales, the majority during September and October.

Sabine's Gull is exceptional in having a complete moult in early spring (prior to the northwards migration), and a partial one in autumn (after arrival in winter quarters); this timing of the moults is the reverse of other gulls, which have a complete moult in autumn and a partial one in spring. Unlike other gulls, too, which start the post-juvenile moult at or shortly after fledging, full juvenile plumage is retained throughout the first autumn until arrival in the southern wintering areas, where the post-juvenile head and body moult to first-winter plumage takes place during November and December. This is followed by a complete moult during the following

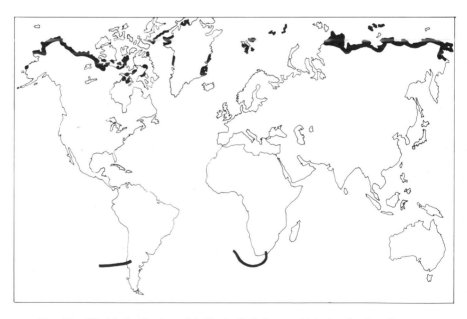

Fig. 39.   World distribution of **Sabine's Gull** *Larus sabini*, showing breeding range (solid black) and approximate southern limit of winter/non-breeding range of Nearctic population off southwest Africa, and of Siberian population off west coast of South America. Scarce in Britain and Ireland, with average of about 15–30 records annually, mainly in southwest in autumn.

February to April, from first-winter to an adult-like first-summer plumage. I am indebted to Piet Meeth for providing an invaluable series of photographs which complemented museum and other photographic evidence, and which is the only material I have located to indicate the appearance of first-winter plumage (Photos 291, 292) and to confirm the extent and timing of the complete moult to first-summer plumage (Photo 293).

Sabine's Gull is between Little Gull and Kittiwake in size, with a forked tail-shape which is difficult to discern except at close range. Its shape in flight resembles a scaled-down Kittiwake, although (largely a function of its smaller size) it has a more buoyant, tern-like flight, making less confident or powerful progress. In flight at all ages, it has a sharply-contrasting, tri-coloured wing pattern, at close range rendering confusion impossible. At long range, however, in the illusory conditions of sea-watches, a major pitfall is provided by first-year Kittiwakes (or possibly even first-year Little Gulls), on which the blackish carpal bar is sometimes impossible to discern, giving a wing pattern which can appear very similar to that of Sabine's, although never matching its actually very striking and clear-cut contrasts of black, grey (greyish-brown on juveniles), and white, the latter almost separating the black and grey near the carpal joint. Caution over this potential identification trap is always advisable, never more than in northern seas in winter when, apart perhaps from the occasional straggler, Sabine's Gulls should be in equatorial and southern oceans (see map, Fig. 39).

Juveniles (which make up the majority of autumn records in Europe) have extensive greyish-brown on the head and breast-sides, giving an almost wholly dark appearance to the bird's front end at long range, when this, combined with the diagnostic wing pattern, is perhaps the best means of distinguishing juvenile Sabine's Gull from juvenile and first-winter Kittiwake, which appears mainly white-headed. At close range, the scaly, greyish-brown mantle, scapulars and coverts of inner wing, dusky bar on the inner underwing, and pale legs (usually blackish on Kittiwake) are diagnostic. Individuals in first-winter plumage are presumably most unlikely to occur in northern seas; they retain the juvenile wing pattern, black-banded tail, a presumably variable amount of greyish-brown wing-coverts, and all-black bill, but otherwise have uniform grey upperparts and winter adult-like head pattern. After the complete moult in spring, the first-summer plumage resembles summer adult, except that a full hood is apparently never acquired (the actual extent of the black on the head is highly variable, often with a partial hood or blackish half-collar on the nape, and smudges below this onto the sides of the neck). Other, less obvious differences of first-summer plumage are in the detailed description. The small number of records of first-summer plumage in Europe suggests that the majority of birds of this age remain in or near the southern wintering areas, and do not return north with the adults in spring. Adults have uniform grey upperparts and coverts of inner wing, a prominent, clear-cut yellow bill-tip, all-white tail, and (in summer) a full black hood or (in winter) black head markings typically confined to a patch or half-collar on the nape.

AGEING SUMMARY

Juvenile: extensive grey-brown on head and breast-sides; scaly, grey-brown upper-parts and coverts of inner wing, black tail-band (summer to December).

First-winter: as adult winter, except for variable amount of retained juvenile inner wing-coverts, black tail band, and all-black bill (November to April).

First-summer: as adult summer, but hood incomplete and usually some other signs of immaturity such as smaller white tips on primaries and/or small, subterminal dark marks on tertials and tail. Yellow bill-tip usually smaller (March to September).

Second-winter: as adult winter, except sometimes traces of immaturity on wings and tail as on first-summer: most are probably indistinguishable from adults in the field (August to April).

Adult summer/second-summer: full hood, immaculate grey upperparts and inner wing-coverts, white tail, black bill with clear-cut yellow tip (March to October).

Adult winter/third-winter: as adult summer, but black on head confined to patch or half-collar on nape (September to March).

DETAILED DESCRIPTIONS

Juvenile (Figs. 34c, 40a and 40b)
HEAD Forehead, narrow eye-ring, lores, chin and throat white. Eye-crescent blackish, remainder of head grey-brown with thin whitish feather fringes.
BODY Mantle, back and scapulars grey-brown, larger feathers with blackish subterminal crescents and neat, whitish or gingery fringes giving scaly effect most prominent on scapulars. Underparts and rump white, except for extensive grey-brown on breast-sides (extension of mantle colour).
WINGS Coverts of inner wing mainly grey-brown, lesser, median and inner greater coverts with blackish subterminal crescents and whitish or gingery fringes giving scaly patterns as on scapulars. Tertials and innermost secondaries grey-brown with clear-cut white fringes, remainder of secondaries and outermost greater coverts white. Alula and most of coverts of outer wing black, inner coverts of outer wing white. Six outer primaries black on outer web with small white tips from 3rd, 4th or 5th inwards; remainder of primaries white, except for blackish of variable extent on outer web of 6th and sometimes also at base of 7th. Inner webs of all primaries mainly white, increasing in extent inwards to wholly white on 6th or 7th, visible as white lines on outer upperwing when wing is fully spread. Underwing white except for exposed black tips of outer primaries (which form a thin dark trailing edge to outer wing), and mainly grey greater underwing coverts which form a dusky bar on the inner underwing; white secondaries and inner primaries form a broad, translucent white triangle on the trailing edge of the inner wing, reflecting the upperwing pattern.
TAIL Obviously forked (but appearing square-cut when fully spread), white, with complete, clear-cut black band (and narrow pale terminal fringe) broadest in centre (accentuating the forked tail-shape) and narrowing outwards to terminal spot on inner web (and sometimes outer web) of outer tail feather.
BARE PARTS Iris brown, orbital ring blackish. Bill black, mouth flesh. Legs pinkish- or greyish-flesh.

First-winter (wing, tail and bill much as juvenile, Figs. 34c, 40a and 40b; head and body much as adult winter, Fig. 40e) Acquired by moult of head and body feathers and variable amount of inner wing-coverts, November and December.
As juvenile, except head pattern, upper body and variable amount of coverts of inner wing as adult winter, and black on wings and tail becoming much worn and faded. Legs presumably become dark at this age on some individuals.

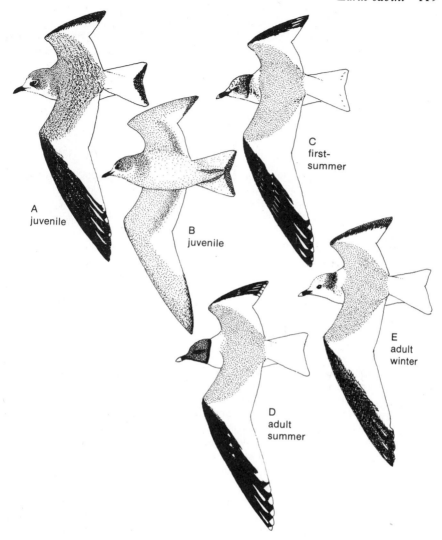

Fig. 40. **Sabine's Gulls** *Larus sabini* in flight.

First-summer (Fig. 40c) Acquired by complete moult, February to April. *As adult summer, except:*

HEAD White with incomplete grey or blackish hood of variable pattern, mainly on ear-coverts and nape, often with blackish half-collar in same position as that on adult, and blackish smudges extending below this onto sides of neck.

WINGS White primary tips smaller, often lacking by late summer through wear; blackish on 6th sometimes more extensive; tertials sometimes with dusky subterminal marks.

TAIL Sometimes a few feathers have subterminal dark marks.

BARE PARTS Yellowish bill tip lacking or smaller and less well-defined. Legs dull flesh or blackish.

Second-winter (upperwing and tail similar to first-summer, Fig. 40C; head as adult winter, 40E) Acquired by head and body moult in autumn, probably August to October.

As first-summer, except head pattern as adult winter, and white on primary tips lacking through wear. Only those which show signs of immaturity on wings and tail are separable from adults.

Adult summer/second-summer (Fig. 40D) Acquired by complete moult, December to April.

HEAD Uniform grey hood (appearing dark or rather pale grey, much depending on light) to nape, bordered along lower edge by complete black collar, broadest on nape. Clear white division between hood and mantle.

BODY Mantle, scapulars and back uniform grey, with thin white scapular- and tertial-crescents. Underparts and rump white.

WINGS Striking, clear-cut, tri-coloured pattern: inner wing-coverts and innermost two or three secondaries mainly uniform grey; remainder of secondaries, most of outer greater coverts, outermost median and lesser coverts, and inner primaries and their coverts white; alula and outer coverts of outer wing black (inner greater primary coverts often with small white tips), and outer five primaries black with large, clear-cut white tips and white tongues on inner webs (the latter visible as white lines on the outer upperwing when wing fully spread). Pattern of black on 6th primary variable, but usually confined to half of outer web and base of inner web. White inner wing-coverts often visible when perched, appearing as white division between grey upperparts and black primaries, merging with white tertial crescents. Underwing white, except for exposed black at tips of outer primaries and faint grey bar on greater underwing coverts; white secondaries and inner primaries form broad, translucent white triangle on trailing edge of inner wing, reflecting upperwing pattern.

TAIL Forked, perhaps more prominently than on juvenile, white.

BARE PARTS Iris blackish-brown, orbital ring red. Bill black with clear-cut, bright yellow tip; mouth and gape reddish. Legs blackish or dark grey.

Adult winter/third-winter (Fig. 40E) Acquired by head and body moult in autumn, probably August to October.

As adult summer, except head white with blackish eye-crescent and variable pattern of blackish-grey, usually confined to fairly defined patch on nape and upper hindneck, but sometimes extending to rear ear-coverts, rear crown, lower hindneck and sides of neck. Outer primaries often brownish and lacking white tips through fading and wear. Bare parts as adult summer, except legs in some colour slides appear to be flesh-coloured or even reddish.

Kittiwake
Rissa tridactyla

(Figs. 35D and 42, Photographs 300–315)

Adult summer

IDENTIFICATION

Kittiwake is between Black-headed and Common Gull *L. canus* in size, with a slightly forked tail-shape (which is usually impossible to detect in the field), very short legs, and rather more upright posture than other gulls when perched. It is an adept marine scavenger, especially around fishing ports and boats at sea, feeding mainly by picking from the surface in flight. In calm conditions, it has a leisurely flight much like other gulls, but in strong winds it adopts a distinctive, powerful flight action which combines deep, stiff wingbeats (with wings sharply angled at the carpal joint) and accomplished shearing (Photo 313).

The differences of first-year Kittiwakes from Sabine's (p. 116) and first-year Little Gulls (p. 107) are described in the respective species accounts.

Juvenile Kittiwake has black bill and legs, black ear-spot and half-collar on the lower hindneck, striking W pattern across the wings in flight, and black tail band. The upperbody is uniform grey like the adult, lacking the brown coloration of other juvenile gulls. First-winter plumage resembles that of the juvenile, except that the half-collar is reduced or lacking, and the bill often begins to acquire pale at the base, and the legs are sometimes dull flesh, occasionally orange-flesh; in first-summer plumage, the wing pattern usually becomes extremely worn and faded.

In second-year plumages, apparently the majority are indistinguishable from adults, but a few are ageable at very close range by one or more immature characters such as a partially black bill, more extensive black on the outer wing, black marks on the tertials, and partial or full winter head pattern in second-summer (not pure white as on summer adults).

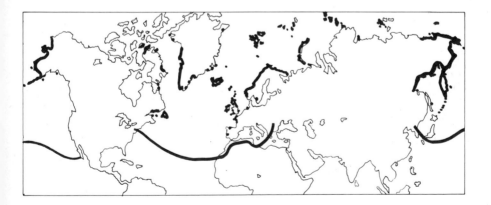

Fig. 41. World distribution of **Kittiwake** *Rissa tridactyla*, showing breeding range (solid black) and approximate southern limit of winter/non-breeding range (black line).

Adults have a white head in summer (dusky markings in winter), white tail, a distinctive flight pattern (dark grey upperparts, mantle and wing-coverts, shading to whitish on the trailing edge and primaries before the clear-cut triangle of black on the wing-tip), greenish-yellow or yellow bill, and black legs.

Juvenile: as first-winter, except black half-collar on lower hindneck always present, and bill always wholly black (summer to October).

First-winter: uniform grey mantle and scapulars, bold blackish W pattern across wings in flight, black tail band, winter head pattern with or without black half-collar, bill sometimes becoming pale at base (August to April).

First-summer: as first-winter, but W pattern faded and much less striking, carpal-bar often reduced, bill usually mainly pale (March to October).

Second-winter and *second-summer:* see detailed descriptions.

Adult winter/second-winter: as adult summer, but head with dusky markings (August to April).

Adult summer/second-summer: white head, underparts and tail, wholly yellowish bill, grey mantle, scapulars and upperwing with clear-cut triangle of black on wing-tip (February to October).

DETAILED DESCRIPTIONS

Juvenile (Fig. 42A. Underwing and tail as first-winter, 42B).
HEAD White, with dusky eye-crescent, blackish ear-spot and broad black half-collar on lower hindneck, remainder of hindneck faintly washed grey.
BODY Mantle, back and scapulars uniform dark grey, latter finely fringed paler. Underparts and rump white.
WINGS Coverts of inner wing dark grey becoming paler outwards, except for clear-cut, broad, blackish carpal-bar; inner greater coverts and tertials broadly edged dark grey. Secondaries white. Alula and outer coverts of outer wing mainly blackish, remainder mainly pale grey. Black on outer web and tip of outer primaries decreasing in extent inwards to subterminal spot on 6th or 7th; small white tips to primaries increasing in size inwards from 5th or 6th. Primaries otherwise pale grey or whitish, with white tongue covering most of inner web from 1st or 2nd inwards. Underwing white, except for exposed black tips of outer primaries (forming a neat, dark trailing edge to outer wing), leading edge of 1st, and speckles on marginal coverts of outer wing.
TAIL White, with clear-cut, black terminal band, broadest in centre (accentuating the slightly forked tail-shape) usually extending to small spot on inner web of outer pair.
BARE PARTS Iris, orbital ring, bill, mouth and legs blackish.

First-winter (Figs. 34D and 42B, from above resembles juvenile, 42A) Acquired by head and body moult, summer to October.

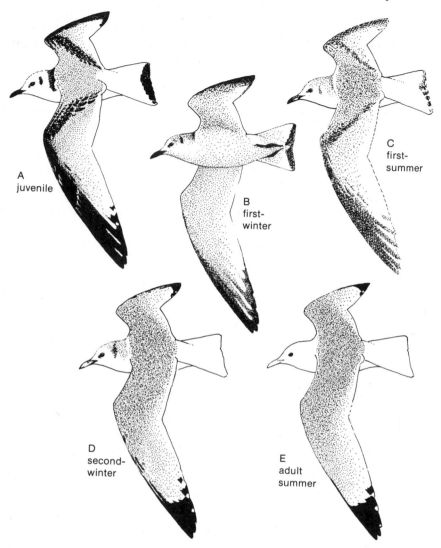

Fig. 42. **Kittiwakes** *Rissa tridactyla* in flight.

As juvenile, except rear crown and hindneck grey, and black half-collar often reduced or replaced by dark grey. Bill sometimes becoming pale at base. Legs usually blackish, but sometimes partially or wholly dull-flesh to orange-flesh, rarely bright pink or orange-red.

First-summer (Fig. 42C depicts a particularly worn and faded individual in late summer. Underwing and tail similar to first-winter, 42B) Acquired by moult of head and body feathers and usually some coverts on inner wing, February to May. *As first-winter, except:*

HEAD Half-collar and ear-spot sometimes lacking.

WINGS Becoming much worn and faded, especially by late summer: carpal-bar reduced in extent and faded to pale brown, and black on outer wing much faded and pattern less defined.

TAIL Black band faded and often reduced by wear.

BARE PARTS Bill often extensively pale yellowish.

Adult winter/second-winter (resembles adult summer, Fig. 42E, but with dusky head markings much as second-winter, 42D) Acquired by complete moult, June to October.

As adult summer, except rear crown and hindneck grey (extension of mantle colour), merging with ill-defined, often crescentic, dark grey or blackish ear-spot which often extends upwards over rear of crown; ill-defined, small dusky eye-crescent.

Probably most second-winter birds are indistinguishable from adults, but at close range some are ageable by one or more immature characters, such as more black on wing-tip, extending to subterminal marks on 6th, rarely 7th or even 8th primaries, and up outer web of 2nd, rarely also 3rd, primaries; outer median and greater primary coverts, or alula occasionally with small black marks; grey on upperwing subtly less 'clean' and uniform, appearing marginally paler and rather patchy; bill often has yet to acquire full adult coloration, retaining some black of highly variable pattern (Fig. 42D).

Adult summer/second-summer (Fig. 42E) Acquired by head and body moult, February to May.

HEAD White.

BODY Mantle, scapulars and back dark grey, obviously darker than Common Gull, with thin white scapular- and tertial-crescents. Underparts and rump white.

WINGS Coverts of inner wing dark grey as mantle, shading to white on trailing edge and to whitish immediately before black of wing-tip. Black on wing-tip confined to outer web of 1st primary, and to clear-cut triangle on inner and outer webs of outer four primaries; subterminal black area on 5th and sometimes also 6th; tiny white tip on 4th increasing in extent inwards. Underwing white, except for black on wing-tip as on upperwing, and pale grey marginal coverts of outer wing.

TAIL White.

BARE PARTS Iris blackish-brown, orbital ring orange-red or red. Bill greenish-yellow or yellow, sometimes whitish at tip; mouth and gape orange. Legs blackish or dark grey. An apparently very rare variant has legs partially or wholly yellow, orange, pink or red.

Most second-summers are indistinguishable from adults, but some show one or more of the immature characters described for second-winter, and some also retain partial or full winter head pattern throughout the summer.

Ivory Gull
Pagophila eburnea
(Figs. 35E and 44, Photographs 316–322)

Adult summer

IDENTIFICATION

Ivory Gull is slightly larger than Common Gull, but more stockily built, with shorter neck, plumper body, and short, strongly-built legs and feet which frequently hang down in flight. On the ground, its full chest, short legs and rolling gait give it an appearance recalling a pigeon *Columba*. The white plumage accentuates its graceful, long-winged flight-jizz. Most commonly it is a scavenger on carrion, but it may also pick food from the surface in flight, often pattering its feet on the surface. It is strong and aggressive, and often more than a match for larger gulls. Contrary to the impression given by most literature, it swims readily.

At all ages, Ivory Gull has a totally distinctive appearance. The 'ermine' pattern of white with black spots of first-year plumages is subject to a great deal of individual variation in the size and distribution of the black spots: those on the primary tips, tail and coverts of outer wing are always present and invariably the most easily visible at a distance, as is the dusky 'face' of juvenile and first-winter birds. The base of the pale-tipped bill is blackish on juveniles, paling to greyish by the first winter. The legs and feet are blackish at all ages.

Adult plumage is acquired in the second winter, a surprisingly short period of immaturity for a gull of this size. Adults in summer and winter have all-white plumage (actually very faintly ivory-toned when viewed against snow); sight of the greyish bill with yellow and orange tip, and the black legs is essential to rule out the slight risk of confusion with wholly albino gulls.

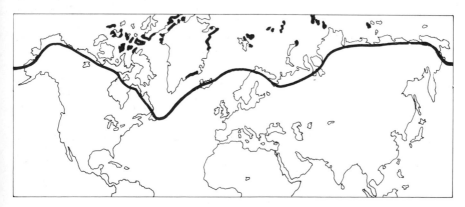

Fig. 43. World distribution of **Ivory Gull** *Pagophila eburnea*, showing approximate breeding range (solid black) and approximate southern limit of winter/non-breeding range (black line). Rare south of Arctic seas, with one or two records annually in Britain and Ireland.

AGEING SUMMARY

Juvenile: as first-winter, but more black spots on head, mantle, scapulars and breast; base of bill blackish (summer to September).

First-winter: white with dusky 'face' and variable amount of black spotting on wings, upperparts and tail band. Bill greyish with yellowish tip (August to April).

First-summer: as first-winter, but dusky 'face' reduced or lacking, and black spotting on upperparts and coverts of inner wing reduced or lacking (March to September).

Adult winter/second-winter: plumage wholly white. Bill greyish with yellow and orange tip (August to April).

Adult summer/second-summer: as adult winter (March to September).

DETAILED DESCRIPTIONS

Juvenile (wings and tail as first-winter, Figs. 35E and 44A).
As first-winter, except crown, nape, hindneck, ear-coverts, mantle, scapulars, and occasionally breast sparsely spotted with black. Base of bill blackish, tip yellowish.

First-winter (Figs. 34E and 44A) Acquired by head and body moult, summer to September.
HEAD White, with grey or blackish 'face' of variable extent on forehead, lores and chin, often extending behind eye. White eye-ring usually prominent in front of eye. Occasionally, a very few spots on crown and nape.
BODY White, with variable amount of black spotting on mantle, scapulars and (rarely) breast.
WINGS White: inner wing with small black subterminal spots on greater, median and lesser coverts (number of spotted feathers varies individually); secondaries white, with or without small black subterminal spots (majority have spots on at least outer secondaries); tertials with usually prominent subterminal black crescents. On outer wing, alula and lesser, median and greater primary coverts have small subterminal black spots. Primaries tipped with black crescentic marks of variable size, decreasing in size inwards to small subterminal marks on 5th to 10th. Underwing white, except for exposed black tips of primaries and secondaries, and dusky marks on marginal coverts of outer underwing.
TAIL White, with black subterminal bars or crescents on all feathers of variable thickness, forming thin, often broken tail band. Uppertail-coverts with or without small, black subterminal spots.
BARE PARTS Iris brown, orbital ring black. Bill grey or grey-green with yellowish or fleshy-yellow tip, sometimes a suggestion of orange at tip of lower mandible. Legs blackish or grey.

First-summer (wings and tail much as first-winter, Figs. 35E and 44A) Acquired by head and body moult, January to May.
As first-winter, except dusky 'face' reduced or lacking, and black spotting on head, mantle, scapulars, and coverts of inner wing reduced or lacking. Bill coloration often as adult.

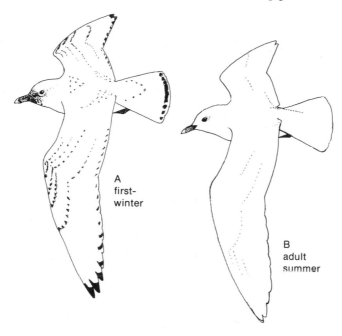

Fig. 44. **Ivory Gulls** *Pagophila eburnea* in flight.

Adult winter/second-winter (as adult summer, Fig. 44B) Acquired by complete moult, May to August.

Whole plumage uniformly white with very faint ivory tone. Shafts of primaries and tail feathers straw-yellow. Iris brown, orbital ring red. Basal two-thirds of bill blue-grey or grey-green, remainder yellowish with orange at tip of lower mandible of variable strength and extent, occasionally lacking. Bill rarely all-yellow. Mouth and gape flesh or orange-flesh. Legs blackish.

Adult summer/second-summer (Fig. 44B) Acquired by head and body moult, January to April.

Much as adult winter, but bill coloration brighter.

Glaucous, Iceland, Sooty and White-eyed Gulls

Glaucous Gull *Larus hyperboreus* and Iceland Gull *L. glaucoides*

The Glaucous Gull (Fig. 46) is rare in most of Europe, but is of sufficiently regular occurrence in northern latitudes (including southern Britain) to make worthwhile a check for its presence among any gatherings of large gulls, especially during November to March. Identification is usually straightforward, but infrequent so-called small individuals (which may not be pure Glaucous Gulls) may give problems, and the possible occurrence of leucistic or albinistic examples of Great Black-backed Gull *L. marinus*, and of hybrid Glaucous × Herring Gull *L. argentatus* needs to be borne in mind. Iceland Gull (Fig. 48) does not breed in the western Palearctic, and is perhaps ten times rarer in Europe than Glaucous Gull, and perhaps only slightly more likely to occur than leucistic or albinistic examples of other species (especially Herring Gull) which have not infrequently been misidentified as Iceland Gulls. These statistics should be remembered when a possible Iceland Gull is encountered: they call for a more cautious approach to identification than has generally been the case in recent years, especially when distant or single fly-by views are involved. The identification problems, however, should not be over-exaggerated: given reasonable views of a typical Iceland Gull, identification is usually straightforward.

IDENTIFICATION

Because the two species are similar at all ages, and because there is no consistent difference in the progression of immature plumages, it is convenient to discuss their identification together, under appropriate headings.

Table 6: Measurements (mm) of **Glaucous** Larus hyperboreus *and* **Iceland Gulls** L glaucoides *(from Dwight 1925)*

	sample	wing	tail	bill	tarsus
Glaucous Gull	21	430–477	180–210	56–67	64–77
Iceland Gull	13	378–433	156–178	39–45	52–63

A
Glaucous

B
Iceland

Fig. 45. First-winter **Glaucous** *Larus hyperboreus* and **Iceland Gulls** *L. glaucoides*, showing comparative sizes and structure.

Plumage: Glaucous and Iceland Gulls are the only large western Palearctic gulls which lack black or blackish on the wings and tail at all ages. First- and second-years in fresh plumage look rather uniformly coffee-coloured or pale grey-brown at a distance: the complex pattern of barring on the upperparts, wings and tail are usually visible only at close range. First-years appear very uniformly coloured on the head and underparts, lacking the distinct streaking or mottling of first-years of other large gulls. At all ages, the whitish primaries and secondaries are a prominent feature in flight, especially when viewed from below, when they appear wholly translucent. There is apparently no consistent plumage difference between the two species at any age, but, on average, first-year Icelands have a neater pattern of barring on the wings and uppertail- and undertail-coverts; generally greyer-brown, less coffee-coloured appearance; and more prominent and broader whitish terminal fringe to the tail. The first-year plumages of both species show a good deal of individual variation in the darkness and pattern of plumage.

Size: The size of most Glaucous Gulls is from that of a large Herring Gull to that of an average Great Black-backed Gull. There is very little size overlap with Iceland Gull, which is typically slightly smaller than an average Herring Gull. Thus, for practical field purposes, size is, by itself, a valid distinction for individuals which are obviously at least as large as the largest Herring Gull (thus Glaucous), or obviously smaller than an average Herring Gull (thus Iceland). For birds which are not side-by-side with other relevant species (and thus do not allow an accurate size assessment), or those which are about the size of an average Herring Gull, structure and (on first-years) bill pattern should be checked.

Structure: A typical Glaucous Gull has a long, heavy, often massive bill, and a long, rather flat-profiled contour to the forehead and crown; bill and head shape combine to give a strong, aggressive look. Iceland Gull has a comparatively short bill (but still occasionally as large as that of a small Herring Gull), more rounded profile to the forehead and crown, and a proportionately slightly larger and more centrally placed eye: these features combine to give a more gentle expression, even recalling that of a Common Gull *L. canus* at times. A useful general rule is that Iceland Gulls' bill is less than half its head length, whereas that of Glaucous is greater, but this may be complicated by the effect on apparent head length which different postures may produce. Perhaps the best impression of the bill size/head shape differences can be obtained by studying the series of photographs of the two species included here.

The whole build of Glaucous is typically   ore massive, with large, full-chested body; bunched tertials and secondaries 'fuller' and bulkier; and proportionately slightly longer legs. Iceland Gull resembles a long-winged small or average Herring Gull in general build, and never gives the very large, bulky impression of a typical Glaucous.

When perched, the projection of the primaries beyond the tail is a good distinction: on Glaucous the projection is comparatively short, always the same or less than the bill length (from the forwardmost extension of feathering on the upper mandible to the tip), whereas on Iceland the projection is obviously much longer than its bill length. This distinction applies throughout the first year and on older individuals which have not dropped or partially regrown the outermost primaries during the complete autumn/winter moult.

On typical Glaucous, the larger size and bulkier structure is obvious in flight, when it looks broad-winged, full-chested and lumbering, with heavy head and bill prominent. Iceland Gull is more elegantly proportioned, with longer, slimmer wings and relatively smaller head and bill. Even so, these structural differences are often very difficult to assess, especially on lone birds.

The structural differences are obvious on typical birds, but on individuals which are indeterminate on size alone, the structural differences, too, may be contentious: bill size and shape, and primary projection are then usually the most reliable structural characters.

Bill pattern: On first-years there is a diagnostic difference in bill pattern. Glaucous Gull always has the basal two-thirds bright flesh-pink to yellowish-cream and a clear-cut black tip extending very slightly, if at all, back along the cutting edges; this bill pattern is not shared by any other first-year large gull, and it is often the first feature by which Glaucous can be located among perched flocks. Iceland Gull has a slightly variable bill pattern, typically with at most the basal half of the bill dull flesh or greyish and an extensive black tip which usually shades into the pale base and extends back in a wedge along the cutting edges. At long range (especially on juveniles and first-winters), the bill may look wholly dark, which is never the case on Glaucous. The bill pattern difference holds good throughout the first year at least (after which the black area usually begins to diminish and the distinctions become lost), but may be evident on some individuals well into the second year.

Identification pitfalls: The possibility of leucistic or albinistic examples of other large gulls (most frequently Herring Gulls), or hybrids (usually Glaucous × Herring Gull), needs to be eliminated when identifying Glaucous and Iceland Gulls. The simple rule is that true or pure Glaucous or Iceland Gulls will never show any characters such as a tail band which is obviously darker than the general coloration of the rest of the plumage; a bar on the secondaries which is darker than the rest of the inner wing; a prominent blackish area around the eye or on the ear-coverts; or outer primaries (on immatures) darker than the inner ones or (on adults) with dark markings, however small, near the wing-tip. Typically, the primaries on Glaucous and Iceland are the palest part of the wing, but on some dark immatures they are as dark as the remainder. Immature leucistic or albinistic gulls invariably have normal bill coloration, and will thus lack the distinctive bill pattern of first-year and some second-year Glaucous and Iceland Gulls; adults, too, have normally coloured bare parts. The presence of one or any combination of these anomalous plumage or bill-pattern characters is a certain indication of leucism or hybridity.

Reference in some literature to an all-white second-year plumage for Glaucous and Iceland Gulls is misleading. Some faded second-years or even first-years may appear white at a distance, but close examination will reveal at least a trace of the normal barring of these ages (especially on areas which are less susceptible to fading such as the undertail-coverts, lower scapulars, or underwing), and normal bill coloration. Any large gull which is genuinely all-white is a certain albino, and then the only clues to identity are usually the bill pattern (on immatures), bare parts colours (on adults), or general size and structure. The difficulty of judging size on any lone bird, and the illusory effects of all-white plumage on apparent size, wing shape and jizz, render even an albino (or leucistic) medium-sized species (such as Common Gull) subject to misidentification as Iceland Gull in brief fly-by views.

Another pitfall is provided by adult Herring Gulls which have moulted or only partially regrown the outer two or three primaries during September to November, towards the end of the complete autumn moult. On such birds, the only black visible on the upperside of the wing-tip in flight is the usually small amount of the 4th and 5th primaries, which is difficult to discern at long range. The extensive black on the partially grown 1st to 3rd primaries is however, usually evident along the leading edge of the outer wing when viewed from below.

Kumlien's Iceland Gull and Thayer's Gull: The likely future occurrence in Europe of Kumlien's Iceland Gull *L. g. kumlieni* (treated here as a subspecies of Iceland Gull, but also variously considered to be a separate species *L. kumlieni*, or a hybrid population of Iceland × Thayer's Gull) or even Thayer's Gull *L. thayeri* (treated here as a separate species in accordance with current AOU opinion, but variously considered to be a subspecies of Herring Gull *L. argentatus thayeri*, a subspecies of Iceland Gull *L. g. thayeri*, or a hybrid population of Kumlien's Iceland × Herring Gull) should be mentioned here. There have been several claims of Kumlien's Iceland Gull in Europe, but apparently none has been officially accepted. Both breed in Arctic Canada, wintering in North America, whereas Iceland Gull winters in Europe (Fig. 48).

Adult and immature Kumlien's Iceland Gulls resemble Iceland Gull, except that first-years average darker, especially on the wings and tail, and (on juveniles and first-winters at least) the bill is all-black; adults have a highly variable pattern of dark grey, occasionally blackish, and prominent clear-cut white tips, on the outer two to five primaries, confined to the outer webs except near the tips, and occasionally have a dark iris. Adult and immature Thayer's Gulls resemble Kumlien's Iceland Gull, except that first-years are darker still, the brown coloration on the outer primaries and almost wholly dark tail being obviously darker than the rest of the upperparts (but not blackish as on Herring Gull); a typical adult has a dark iris, and a wing-tip pattern of blackish intermediate in extent between Herring Gull and Kumlien's Iceland Gull, thus blackish, occasionally dark grey, of variable pattern, often extending onto the inner webs.

This group shows a cline from the palest immatures/whitest adult wing-tips to the darkest immatures/blackest adult wing-tips, thus Iceland–Kumlien's Iceland–Thayer's–Herring. There is considerable overlap, but only between adjacent components of the cline, so that some individuals are not assignable with certainty. The most recent discussions on the complex taxonomic and identification problems of the group are by Gosselin and David (1975) and Lehman (1980), on which parts of this summary are based, and which are an essential reference. It would seem, however, that claims of either in Europe are likely to be clouded by the complication of hybrid Herring × Glaucous Gulls (or even the possibility of Herring × Iceland Gulls) which show a restricted and variable extent of black on the wing-tip, or (in the case of a claimed Thayer's Gull) by the not infrequent occurrence of Herring Gulls—probably mainly of the Scandinavian subspecies *L. a. argentatus*—which have a reduced amount of black on the wing-tip, thus having a Thayer's-like pattern. Perhaps the best chance is with a typical adult Kumlien's Gull, on which the correct wing-tip pattern of dark grey would be difficult to explain away by hybridity.

AGEING SUMMARY

The difficulties of accurately ageing a proportion of immature large gulls after their first year (see pages 69–70) apply equally to Glaucous and Iceland Gulls. There is a further complication in that there is more individual variation in the strength of the dark patterning of juveniles than in the cases of other large gulls. This, combined with the fact that their paler plumage is more prone to fading, means that what started out as 'pale-morph' juveniles can appear very whitish in first-winter (from as early as January) and first-summer plumages, and at long range they may be difficult to separate from the normal, pale, less barred and often whitish plumage of second-years. Thus, during January to April (after which second-summers are usually obvious as such by at least some clear grey on the upperparts), it is safest to leave the age of pale buff or whitish individuals as indeterminate (i.e. 'first- or second-winter', or 'first- or second-summer'), unless views are close enough to determine the age-diagnostic characters of most second-years, such as a pale iris, smaller extent of black on the bill-tip (with prominent pale area at extreme tip), less prominently barred wings (especially the greater coverts and tertials), presence of any clear grey on the mantle and/or scapulars, or the slightly rounded outer primary tips and square-tipped tail feathers (pointed and rounded respectively on first-years). Extremely worn primaries, on which the tips are sharply pointed or on which only the shafts remain at the tips are typical of some late first-winters and most first-summers; such extreme wear is never evident on second-years.

Juvenile: whole plumage fresh and unworn. Head and underparts rather uniform brown. Mantle and scapulars neatly patterned. Wing-coverts neatly barred. First-year bill pattern (summer to October).

First-winter: as juvenile, except head and underparts averaging paler, and mantle and scapulars more coarsely patterned (September to March).

First-summer: as first-winter, except head and underparts usually very pale or whitish, mantle and scapulars often whitish with coarse dark barring, and wing-coverts very pale or whitish through wear. Wings and tail very worn (March to September).

Second-winter: whole plumage generally whitish or generally paler and more uniform, less barred, than juvenile/first-winter. Head and underparts sometimes rather coarsely streaked. Bill much as first-year, but usually with obvious pale area at extreme tip. Iris usually becoming pale (August to March).

Second-summer: as second-winter, but whole plumage generally faded paler or whitish. Mantle and scapulars with variable amount of clear grey. Iris pale (March to September).

Third-winter: as adult winter, except grey or upperparts and wings patchy with some faint brownish markings on coverts, often some duskiness on tail, and usually small subterminal blackish markings on bill (October to April).

Third-summer: as third-winter, except head and underparts white (February to September).

Adult winter/fourth-winter: head heavily streaked; upperparts and wings uniform grey; tail all-white; adult bill pattern (November to March).

Adult summer/fourth-summer: as adult winter, except head white (February to September).

DETAILED DESCRIPTIONS

For Glaucous Gull see overleaf: for Iceland Gull see page 138.

Glaucous Gull
Larus hyperboreus

(Figs. 45A and 47, Photographs 323–343)

Adult summer

Juvenile (similar to first-winter, Figs. 45A and 47A)

HEAD Rather uniform light brownish-grey or buff, shading to whitish on chin and around base of bill. Streaking fine and inconspicuous. Eye-crescent dusky; whitish crescents above and below eye.

BODY Underparts uniform brownish-grey or buff, usually darkest on belly, with mottles or faint bars especially on breast-sides and flanks; underparts often generally darker than upperparts. Mantle and scapulars pale buff with intricate, neat pattern of brownish bars or chevrons of variable strength, with barring strongest on lower scapulars. Rump strongly barred.

WINGS Coverts of inner wing pale buff with neat pattern of dark bars, but greater coverts more strongly and coarsely marked (pattern highly variable), but becoming progressively more uniform grey-brown outwards. Tertials coarsely patterned as inner greater coverts. Primaries and secondaries mainly uniform grey-brown or buff (as dark or paler than general colour of rest of wing) with broad whitish tips and fringes which combine to form strikingly whitish wing point when perched, dusky subterminal mottling or chevrons of variable pattern and strength, and whitish or straw-coloured shafts. Underwing-coverts and axillaries mottled with dark, of similar general coloration to underparts.

TAIL Typically rather plain pale grey or buff, with highly variable marbled or 'watered' pattern of whitish and dark mottles and bars. Uppertail- and undertail-coverts strongly barred.

BARE PARTS Iris dark brown. Basal two-thirds of bill bright flesh-pink to pale flesh, with sharply-demarcated black tip; mouth flesh. Legs pale flesh.

Fig. 46.   World distribution of **Glaucous Gull** *Larus hyperboreus*, showing approximate breeding range (solid black) and approximate southern limits of winter/non-breeding range (black line).

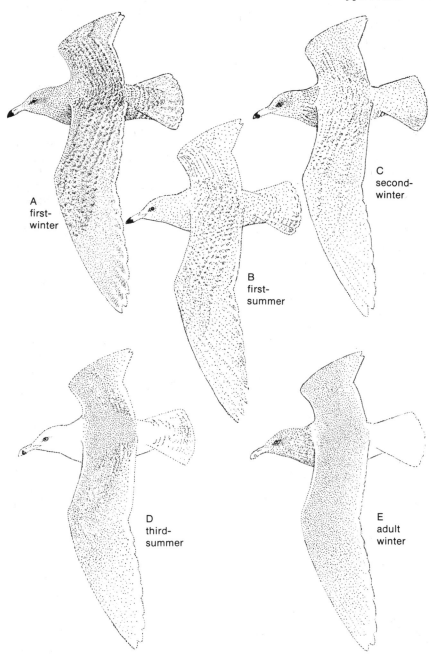

A
first-
winter

B
first-
summer

C
second-
winter

D
third-
summer

E
adult
winter

Fig. 47. **Glaucous Gulls** *Larus hyperboreus* in flight.

First-winter (Figs. 45A and 47A) Acquired by post-juvenile head and body moult, summer to October.

As juvenile, except head and underparts averaging slightly paler, and mantle and scapulars basically whiter, usually with coarser, more irregular pattern of bars; sometimes indistinguishable from juvenile plumage. From January onwards, some become worn and faded, acquiring generally whitish appearance as moult to first-summer progresses.

First-summer (Fig. 47B) Acquired by head and body moult, January to May.

As first-winter, except head and body very pale buff or whitish, with faint mottling or streaking, and mantle and scapulars whitish, with irregular, often sparse brown barring which may become inconspicuous through fading. Wings and tail becoming much worn and faded, in extreme cases acquiring very whitish appearance as base colour fades and dark juvenile markings become faint or disappear. Bill often acquires small pale area at extreme tip, and yellowish-flesh at base.

Second-winter (Fig. 47C) Acquired by complete moult, April to September. *As first-winter, except:*

HEAD AND BODY Head and underparts basically pale buff or whitish, sometimes rather coarsely streaked or mottled, less uniform. Mantle and scapulars basically paler buff or whitish, with sparse, less intricate pattern of barring.

WINGS Generally pale buff and plainer, without neat, defined barring on coverts and tertials; greater coverts mainly plain pale buff or whitish, with patterning much finer and paler, usually confined to innermost. Tertials as inner greater coverts. Underwing mainly dusky, similar to underparts. Primaries and secondaries plainer; pale buff or whitish.

TAIL Typically more uniform and paler, with fainter markings. Uppertail- and undertail-coverts less strongly barred.

BARE PARTS Iris occasionally pale at this age. Black on bill usually less extensive, extreme tip usually obviously pale, and base pink, yellowish or yellowish-flesh.

Second-summer (not illustrated, but plumage similar to second-summer Iceland Gull, Fig. 49C) Acquired by head and body moult, January to May.

As second-winter, except head and underparts pale buff or whitish. Mantle and scapulars invariably with some clear grey or whitish grey, usually extensive. Wings and tail acquiring uniform whitish or very pale pale buff appearance through wear and fading. Iris pale, sometimes obvious only at close range; orbital ring sometimes yellowish. Bill pattern as second-winter or with thick, subterminal dark band.

Third-winter (not illustrated, but plumage similar to third-winter Icelánd Gull, Fig. 48D) Acquired by complete moult, April to January.

HEAD As adult winter.

BODY Underparts white or with some brownish mottling. Mantle and scapulars mainly clear pale grey. Rump white or faintly mottled.

WINGS As adult, but grey patchy, not uniform, with faint brownish freckling especially on inner greater coverts and tertials; primaries sometimes whitish, without clear grey. Underwing white or faintly mottled.

TAIL White, usually with faint brownish freckling; uppertail and undertail-coverts sometimes faintly barred.

BARE PARTS As adult except bill with usually obvious blackish subterminal marks, and sometimes lacking red on gonys.

Third-summer (Fig. 47D) Acquired by head and body moult, January to April. As third-winter, except head and underparts white or faintly streaked.

Adult winter/fourth-winter (Fig. 47E) Acquired by complete moult, July to February.

HEAD White, with often dense brownish or orange-brown streaking confined to head and upper breast. Eye-crescent dusky; whitish crescent above and below eye.

BODY Underparts and rump white. Upperparts uniform pale grey, slightly paler than those of Herring Gull *L. a. argenteus*, with prominent white scapular- and tertial-crescents when perched.

WINGS Upperwing pale grey with thin white leading edge and broad white trailing edge. Primaries and secondaries broadly tipped white; shafts straw-coloured. Underwing white.

TAIL White.

BARE PARTS Iris pale yellow; orbital ring yellowish. Bill yellowish with orange-red spot near gonys and whitish at extreme tip.

Individuals as adult, except for small black subterminal mark on bill and with patchy grey and whitish upperparts are probably fourth-years.

Adult summer/fourth-summer (not illustrated, but plumage similar to adult summer Iceland Gull, Fig. 49E) Acquired by head and body moult, January to March.

As adult winter, except head and underparts white, and yellow and red on bill brighter.

Iceland Gull
Larus glaucoides

(Figs. 45B and 49, Photographs 344–356)

Adult summer

Juvenile (similar to first-winter, Figs. 45B and 49A)
Description as for juvenile Glaucous Gull, except: general coloration greyer-brown, less buff or coffee-coloured on average; pattern of dark barring on mantle, scapulars and wings neater, denser and less coarse on average; barring on uppertail and undertail-coverts denser and finer on average; dark crescentic mark near tip of each primary more prominent on average; and whitish terminal fringe on tail broader and more prominent on average. Bill pattern slightly variable, typically with at most basal half dull flesh or greyish, and black tip more extensive, usually shading into pale base and extending back in wedge along cutting edges; bill usually appears all dark at long range.

First-winter (Figs. 45B and 49A) Acquired by post-juvenile head and body moult, summer to September.
As first-winter Glaucous Gull.

First-summer (Fig. 49B) Acquired by head and body moult, January to April.
As first-winter Glaucous Gull. Base of bill usually pale flesh.

Second-winter (not illustrated, but plumage similar to second-winter Glaucous Gull, Fig. 47C) Acquired by complete moult, April to September.
As second-winter Glaucous Gull, except some pale grey feathers on mantle and

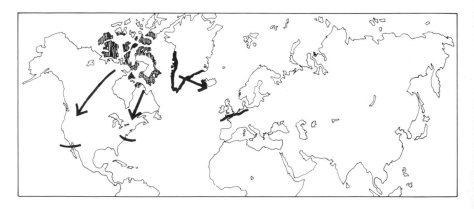

Fig. 48.   Approximate breeding range of **Iceland Gull** *Larus glaucoides* (solid black), **Kumlien's Iceland Gull** *L. g. kumlieni* (spotted), and **Thayer's Gull** *L. thayeri* (hatched), and approximate southern limit of winter/non-breeding range (Iceland in Europe, Kumlien's Iceland mainly in eastern North America, and Thayer's mainly in western North America).

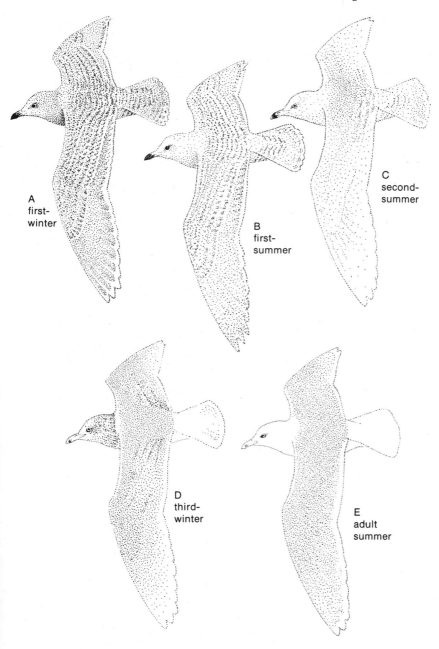

Fig. 49. **Iceland Gulls** *Larus glaucoides* in flight. The first-winter is towards the darkest extreme of variation.

scapulars sometimes acquired at this age. Distinctive first-year bill pattern often retained, but with obvious pale area at extreme tip, or black area reduced so that pattern resembles that of first-year Glaucous.

Second-summer (Fig. 49c) Acquired by head and body moult, January to April. As second-winter Glaucous Gull. Distinctions from Glaucous Gull of first-year bill pattern usually lost by this age.

Third-winter (Fig. 49D); **third-summer** (plumage similar to Glaucous Gull, Fig. 47D); **adult winter/fourth-winter** (plumage similar to adult winter Glaucous Gull, Fig. 47E); and **adult summer/fourth-summer** (Fig. 49E): descriptions and moult timing much as for Glaucous Gull, except orbital ring of breeding adult usually red, not yellowish.

Fig. 50.   First-winter **Sooty** *Larus hemprichii* and **White-eyed Gulls** *L. leucophthalmus*, showing comparative sizes and structure.

Sooty Gull *Larus hemprichii* and **White-eyed Gull** *L. leucophthalmus*

These two Middle East specialities (Figs. 51 & 53) are of medium size, and share rather similar plumage patterns and structural features. At all ages, they have a generally dark coloration, blackish underwings, and long-winged silhouette, which at long range in flight may recall a skua *Stercorarius* or first-year Lesser Black-backed Gull *L. fuscus*. Both have exceptionally long bills and, when perched, long wings which form an elongated rear end; unlike any other western Palearctic gull, the hoods of adults extend as a bib onto the upper breast. These features combine to give the two species a general appearance which is strikingly different from all other western Palearctic gulls.

The following summaries and descriptions are almost entirely based on photographs and museum specimens, and the value of many of the identification and ageing characters requires testing or confirmation in the field.

First- and most second-years are readily ageable. The timing of the breeding season varies greatly for different populations of both species; the timing of the post-juvenile and subsequent moults is fixed by the fledging date, so temporal limits cannot be set for the incidence of the various plumages.

IDENTIFICATION

Sooty Gull is the same size or slightly smaller than Common Gull; White-eyed Gull is slightly smaller, between Black-headed Gull *L. ridibundus* and Common Gull, closest to the latter; the dark coloration and rather languid flight of both species, however, recall immatures of some larger western Palearctic gulls, and on lone birds may give a misleading impression of much larger size.

Sooty Gull has an exceptionally long and thick bill, proportionately much larger and heavier than that of any other western Palearctic gull; the bill of White-eyed is just as long, but slimmer, exaggerating its length. Sooty Gull is generally more heavily built than White-eyed, with broader, less pointed wings in flight. Structure, especially bill shape, is among the best specific differences at all ages.

The plumage of Sooty Gull is generally pale brown on first-years to grey-brown on adults, and the hood of adults is dark brown marked by a prominent white crescent above the eye, and sometimes also a faint white crescent below the eye. The general

Table 7: Measurements in mm of Sooty Larus hemprichii *and White-eyed Gulls* L. leucophthalmus *(from Dwight 1925)*

	sample	wing	tail	bill	tarsus
Sooty Gull	24	318–352	114–132	44–52	48–59
White-eyed Gull	11	305–332	107–125	43–52	44–50

coloration of White-eyed Gull is greyer, less brown, at all ages, and the hood of adults is jet black with very prominent, thick white crescents above and below the eye. Contrary to descriptions in most literature, the iris of White-eyed Gull is dark at all ages, never white. In winter, the head markings of both species are apparently duller or less well-defined, and, according to the literature, the white half-collar on the lower hindneck is sometimes obscured or lacking.

In first-year plumages, Sooty Gull has clear pale fringes on the wing-coverts and tertials, forming an obvious scaly pattern; on White-eyed Gull, these areas are more uniformly brownish, lacking prominent pale fringes. The head pattern of Sooty Gull is rather plain, pale brown, whereas White-eyed has a rather well-defined blackish mask and nape, whitish throat, and ill-defined, fine blackish streaks on the head and breast. Sooty Gull has a greyish bill with sharply contrasting black tip, whereas White-eyed has a wholly black bill. The legs of Sooty Gull are greyish, whereas those of White-eyed Gull are greenish.

Second-years of both species resemble adults, but typically show immature characters such as black or black and grey on the tail of highly variable pattern more extensive blackish bar on the secondaries, paler and less well-defined head pattern, and bare parts lacking full adult colour.

DETAILED DESCRIPTIONS

For Sooty Gull see facing page; for White-eyed Gull see page 146.

Sooty Gull
Larus hemprichii

(Figs. 50A and 52, Photographs 357–369)

Adult summer

Juvenile (not illustrated, but wings and tail similar to first-winter, Figs. 50A and 52A)

HEAD Pale brown, paler than mantle, shading to brown on nape and whitish on chin and face. Whitish crescent above eye. Dark eye-crescent.

BODY Broad breast-band and flanks pale brown with some mottling; belly and undertail-coverts whitish. Mantle and scapulars brown, with pale fringes forming scaly pattern; rump and uppertail-coverts pale grey-brown or whitish.

WINGS Secondaries and outer primaries blackish, inner primaries paler; inner three or four primaries and secondaries fringed and tipped whitish, forming thin white trailing edge to inner wing; tertials pale brown, clearly fringed whitish. Coverts of inner wing pale brown, fringed whitish, forming scaly pattern, and thin whitish lines across tips of greater and median coverts in flight. Underwing wholly grey-brown.

TAIL Mainly black, with thin white terminal fringe and white basally on inner webs of outer feathers; tail thus often appearing wholly black from above, but with very broad subterminal band when fully spread or from below.

BARE PARTS Iris dark brown. Base of bill greyish or blue-grey, tip black. Legs greyish or blue-grey, a shade darker than bill-base.

First-winter (Figs. 50A and 52A) Acquired by post-juvenile head and body moult, probably August to March, depending on fledging-date.

As juvenile, except breast-band and flanks grey-brown, mantle and scapulars grey-brown, rump and uppertail-coverts whitish, and wings and tail becoming worn and faded.

First-summer (similar to first-winter, Figs. 50A and 52A) Acquired by head and body moult, probably March to October.

As first-winter, except wings and tail becoming much worn and faded, wing-coverts and tertials usually losing pale fringes.

Fig. 51. World distribution of **Sooty Gull** *Larus hemprichii*, showing approximate breeding range (solid black) and approximate non-breeding range (spotted). Apparently rare in southeastern Mediterranean.

Second-winter (Fig. 52B) Acquired by complete moult, probably August to May. *As adult winter, except:*

HEAD Usually little different from first-winter.

BODY Mantle, scapulars, breast-band and flanks usually patchy and browner, less uniform grey-brown.

WINGS Blackish bar on secondaries broader and more extensive, white trailing edge on inner wing thinner, and white tips and fringes on inner primaries less prominent and often confined to innermost.

TAIL White, with highly variable pattern of black subterminal marks or black and grey, varying from little different from first-year pattern to subterminal black spots on only one or two pairs of feathers.

BARE PARTS Bill pattern and colour usually little different from that of first-year.

Second-summer (not illustrated, but wings and tail similar to second-winter, Fig. 52B) Acquired by head and body moult, probably March to October.

As second-winter, except hood and bare parts varying from like adult to little different from second-winter.

Adult winter/third-winter (not illustrated, but wings and tail similar to adult summer, Fig. 52C) Acquired by complete moult, probably August to May. *As adult summer, except:*

HEAD Brown of hood paler, and white half-collar less well-defined or occasionally lacking.

WINGS Primaries, primary coverts and alula black, shading to blackish-brown inwards; white tips to primaries from 3rd or 4th, increasing in size inwards to large white tips on innermost. Secondaries and tertials blackish-brown, with white tips forming broad trailing edge to inner wing. Coverts of inner wing uniform dark grey-brown. Underwing dull brown, coverts and axillaries blackish-brown.

BARE PARTS Somewhat duller.

Adult summer/third-summer (Fig. 52C) Acquired by head and body moult, probably March to October.

HEAD Shape of hood unlike any other western Palearctic gull except White-eyed, covering whole head and extended to narrow rounded bib on upper breast; hood very dark brown (looking black at distance), shading to blackish on lower nape and bib. White crescent above eye invariably prominent, and sometimes also inconspicuous thin white crescent or mark below eye. Hood bordered at nape and sides of neck by white half-collar.

BODY Broad grey-brown breast-band bordering bib, extending onto flanks; belly and undertail-coverts white. Mantle and scapulars uniform brown-washed dark grey; rump and uppertail-coverts white.

WINGS As adult winter, except faded browner, and white primary tips often lacking through wear except on innermost.

TAIL White.

BARE PARTS Iris dark brown; orbital ring red. Bill yellow or greenish-yellow with blackish area or band of variable extent before bright red tip: extreme tip often yellowish. Gape red, mouth flesh. Legs dull yellow or greenish-yellow.

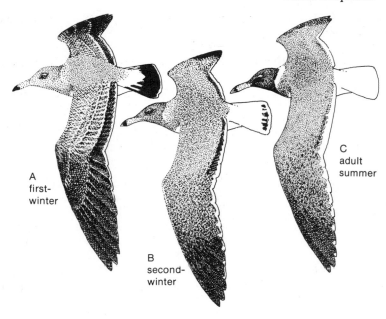

A
first-
winter

B
second-
winter

C
adult
summer

Fig. 52.   **Sooty Gulls** *Larus hemprichii* in flight.

White-eyed Gull
Larus leucophthalmus

(Figs. 50B and 54, Photographs 370–376)

Adult summer

Juvenile (not illustrated, but wings and tail similar to first-winter, Figs. 50B and 54A)

HEAD Brown with whitish face and throat, faintly streaked on crown and around ear-coverts (thus generally darker and less plain than on Sooty Gull); eye-crescent and patch on ear coverts dusky; whitish crescents above and below eye.

BODY Breast-band brownish, narrower than on Sooty Gull, faintly streaked across lower throat, extending to flanks; belly and undertail-coverts whitish. Mantle and scapulars grey-brown, slightly darker and greyer, less brown, than on Sooty Gull, lacking obvious pale feather-fringes; rump and uppertail-coverts greyish.

WINGS Primaries and secondaries blackish, with narrow white trailing edge on secondaries and innermost primaries; tertials grey-brown with inconspicuous pale fringes. Coverts of upperwing mainly grey-brown, with inconspicuous pale fringes, thus lacking prominent scaly pattern as on Sooty Gull. Underwing wholly grey-brown.

TAIL Black, usually lacking any white terminal fringe, with small white area basally on inner web of outer feathers; when tail fully spread, or from below, black terminal band broader than on Sooty Gull, but tail usually appearing wholly black.

BARE PARTS Iris dark brown. Bill glossy black with brownish area at base of lower mandible. Legs greenish-grey.

First-winter (Figs. 50B and 54A) Acquired by post-juvenile head and body moult, probably August to March, depending on fledging date.

As juvenile, except head with more defined blackish mask through eye to nape. Breast-band, flanks and mantle uniform grey-brown, a shade darker and greyer, less brown, than on Sooty Gull.

First-summer (similar to first-winter, Figs. 50B and 54A) Acquired by head and body moult, probably March to October.

As first-winter, except wings and tail becoming much worn and faded.

Fig. 53. World distribution of **White-eyed Gull** *Larus leucophthalmus*, showing approximate breeding range (solid black) and approximate non-breeding range (spotted).

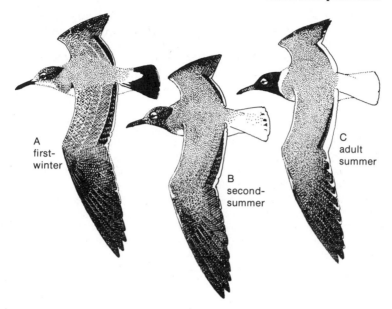

Fig. 54. White-eyed Gulls *Larus leucophthalmus* in flight.

Second-winter (not illustrated, but wings and tail similar to second-summer, Fig. 54B) Acquired by complete moult, probably August to May. *As adult winter, except:*

HEAD Hood and bib basically browner, perhaps often little different from first-winter.

BODY Mantle, scapulars, breast-band and flanks less immaculate grey. Rump usually clouded with grey.

WINGS Outer primaries, coverts and alula blackish, shading to greyer inwards; white fringes at tips of primaries from 7th inwards, less prominent than on Sooty Gull. Secondaries blackish with less broad white trailing edge. Coverts of inner wing a shade browner, less immaculate grey.

TAIL White, or with highly variable pattern of black and grey, usually forming broken subterminal tail band.

BARE PARTS Bill and legs usually duller.

Second-summer (Fig. 54B) Acquired by head and body moult, probably March to October.

As second-winter, except hood and bare parts varying from like adult to little different from second-winter.

Adult winter/third-winter (not illustrated, but wings and tail similar to adult summer, Fig. 54C) Acquired by complete moult, probably August to May. *As adult summer, except:*

HEAD Hood and bib peppered with white flecking; white half-collar less well-defined.

WINGS Primaries and outer primary coverts black, shading to dark grey inwards; white tips to primaries smaller than on Sooty Gull, from 3rd, 4th or 5th increasing in size inwards. Secondaries and tertials blackish with white tips forming broad trailing edge to inner wing. Wing-coverts uniform dark grey. Thin white leading edge to inner wing, usually lacking on Sooty Gull (S. C. Madge *in litt.*). Underwing dull grey-brown, coverts and axillaries blackish-brown.

BARE PARTS Somewhat duller.

Adult summer/third-summer (Fig. 54C) Acquired by head and body moult, probably March to October.

HEAD Shape of hood and bib much as adult summer Sooty Gull, but uniform glossy black, not dark brown, and with prominent, thick white crescents above and below eye. White half collar as on adult Sooty Gull.

BODY Breast-band and flanks pale grey, less extensive than on Sooty Gull; belly and coverts white. Mantle and scapulars dark grey without obvious brownish tone as on Sooty Gull; rump and uppertail-coverts white.

WINGS As adult winter, except white primary tips usually lacking through wear except on innermost.

TAIL White.

BARE PARTS Iris dark brown; orbital ring red. Bill bright red with black tip. Legs bright yellowish.

References

BARTH, E. K. 1975. Taxonomy of *Larus argentatus* and *Larus fuscus* in north-western Europe. *Ornis Scand*. 6: 49–63.

DWIGHT, J. 1925. The Gulls (Laridae) of the World: their plumages, moults, variations, relationships and distribution. *Bull. Amer. Mus. Nat. Hist*. 52: 63–401.

GARCIA, E. F. J. 1977. Field identification of juvenile Audouin's Gull. *Bull. Gibraltar Ornithological Group* 2: 3–6.

GOSSELIN, M., & DAVID, N. 1975. Field identification of Thayer's Gull *Larus thayeri* in eastern North America. *Amer. Birds* 29: 1059–1066.

HUME, R. A. 1978. Variations in Herring Gulls at a Midland roost. *Brit. Birds* 71: 338–345.

―― 1979. Variations in Herring Gulls. *Brit. Birds* 72: 390–392.

LEHMAN, P. 1980. The identification of Thayer's Gull in the field. *Birding* 12: 198–210.

MONAGHAN, P., & DUNCAN, N. 1979. Plumage variation of known-age Herring Gulls. *Brit. Birds* 72: 100–103.

NICOLAU-GUILLAUMET, P. 1977. Mise au point et réflexions sur la répartition des Goélands argentés *Larus argentatus* de France. *Alauda* 45: 53–73.

REE, V. 1973. *Larus cirrocephalus*, nueva especie de gaviota para España y Europa. *Ardeola* 19: 22–23.

SMITH, K. D. 1972. The winter distribution of *Larus audouinii*. *Bull. BOC* 92: 34–37.

VAURIE, C. 1965. *The Birds of the Palearctic Fauna. Non-Passeriformes*. London.

Page index of photographs

1.   Juvenile **Black-headed Gull** *L. ridibundus*, South Yorkshire, July 1970 (Richard Vaughan).

2.   Juvenile **Black-headed Gull** *L. ridibundus*, North Humberside, July 1967 (Richard Vaughan).

3.   **Black-headed Gull** *L. ridibundus*, moulting from juvenile to first-winter, Kent, August 1976 (Pamela Harrison).

4. **Black-headed Gull** *L. ridibundus*, at start of moult from juvenile to first-winter, Gwynedd, August 1979 (R. J. Chandler).

5. **Black-headed Gull** *L. ridibundus*, at start of moult from juvenile to first-winter, Netherlands, July 1980 (Dirk Moerbeek).

6.   First-winter **Black-headed Gull** *L. ridibundus*, North Humberside, February 1971 (Richard Vaughan).

7.   First-winter **Black-headed Gull** *L. ridibundus*, USSR, November 1976 (Pamela Harrison).

8.   **Black-headed Gull** *L. ridibundus*, moulting from first-winter to first-summer, Italy, March 1981 (R. J. Chandler).

9.   **Black-headed Gull** *L. ridibundus*, moulting from first-winter to first-summer, Merseyside, March 1981 (Peter M. Harris).

10, 11. First-summer **Black-headed Gulls** *L. ridibundus*, Kent, April 1976 (Pamela Harrison).

12. (below) First-summer **Black-headed Gull** *L. ridibundus*, Merseyside, May 1981 (Peter M. Harris).

13. **Black-headed Gull** *L. ridibundus*, moulting from first-summer to second-winter, Netherlands, July 1980 (Dirk Moerbeek).

14. Adult **Black-headed Gull** *L. ridibundus*, near end of moult from summer to winter plumage (note outermost primaries still growing), Merseyside, October 1980 (Peter M. Harris).

15. Adult winter **Black-headed Gull** *L. ridibundus*, London, February 1981 (R. J. Chandler).

16. Adult winter **Black-headed Gull** *L. ridibundus*, North Humberside, October 1970 (Richard Vaughan).

17.   Adult winter **Black-headed Gulls** *L. ridibundus*, North Humberside, January 1971. Obvious fine black lines on the outer webs of the outermost primaries, as on the upper left and lower right individuals, are probably an indication of second-winter rather than fully adult plumage (Richard Vaughan).

18.   Adult **Black-headed Gull** *L. ridibundus*, moulting from winter to summer plumage, Avon, February 1979 (Peter M. Harris).

19.   Adult **Black-headed Gull** *L. ridibundus* moulting from winter to summer plumage, London, March 1976 (R. J. Chandler).

20.   Adult summer **Black-headed Gull** *L. ridibundus*, London, February 1977 (R. J. Chandler).

21.   Adult summer **Black-headed Gull** *L. ridibundus*, Sweden, summer 1972 (Bengt Bengtsson).

22.   Adult summer **Black-headed Gull** *L. ridibundus*. Note faded hood and moult to winter plumage just starting, Denmark, July 1971 (Richard Vaughan).

23, 24, 25. First-winter **Slender-billed Gulls** *L. genei*, Bulgaria, September 1976 (Dr Brigitte Königstedt).

26.   First-winter **Slender-billed Gull** *L. genei*, Turkey, October 1977 (S. C. Madge).

27.   Adult winter **Slender-billed Gull** *L. genei*, Iran, February 1971 (Pamela Harrison).

28, 29.   Adult winter **Slender-billed Gulls** *L. genei*, with one adult winter Black-headed Gull *L. ridibundus* (right), Iran, February 1971 (Pamela Harrison).

30. Adult summer **Slender-billed Gull** *L. genei*, France, June 1977 (J. G. Prins).

31. Adult summer **Slender-billed Gull** *L. genei*, USSR (E. Bragin).

32. Adult summer **Slender-billed Gulls** *L. genei*, USSR, May 1976 (V. D. Siokhin)

33, 34. Adult summer **Slender-billed Gulls** *L. genei*, USSR, May 1976 (V. D. Siokhin).

35, 36. Adult summer **Slender-billed Gulls** *L. genei*,
USSR, May 1976 (V. D. Siokhin).

37. Juvenile **Bonaparte's Gull** *L. philadelphia*, USA, August 1980 (E. J. Mackrill).

38. **Bonaparte's Gull** *L. philadelphia* near end of moult from juvenile to first-winter, Canada, September 1979 (Philip Perry).

39. First-winter **Bonaparte's Gull** *L. philadelphia*, USA, March 1975 (Alan Brady).

40. First-winter **Bonaparte's Gull** *L. philadelphia*, Dorset, April 1981 (David M. Cottridge).

41.   First-winter **Bonaparte's Gull** *L. philadelphia*, Dorset, April 1981 (John Miller).

42.   First-winter **Bonaparte's Gull** *L. philadelphia*, Dorset, April 1981 (Phil Vines).

43.   **Bonaparte's Gull** *L. Philadelphia*, moulting from first-summer to second-winter (note remaining black-banded first-year tail), USA, July 1980 (E. J. Mackrill).

44. Adult winter **Bonaparte's Gull** *L. philadelphia*, Canada, September 1979 (Philip Perry).

45. Adult winter **Bonaparte's Gull** *L. philadelphia*, Cornwall, March 1968 (J. B. & S. Bottomley).

46. Adult winter **Bonaparte's Gull** *L. philadelphia*, with adult summer Black-headed Gull *L. ridibundus*, Cornwall, March 1968 (J. B. & S. Bottomley).

47. Adult summer **Bonaparte's Gull** *L. philadelphia*, at start of moult to winter plumage (note missing innermost primaries), Canada, summer 1971 (Alan Kitson).

48. Juvenile **Grey-headed Gull** *L. cirrocephalus*, South Africa (Gerry Nicholls).

49. **Grey-headed Gull** *L. cirrocephalus*, near end of moult from juvenile to first-winter, Peru, June 1981 (E. J. Mackrill).

50.   First-winter **Grey-headed Gull** *L. cirrocephalus*, Peru, January 1981 (E. J. Mackrill)

51. Second-winter **Grey-headed Gull** *L. cirrocephalus*, Peru, June 1981 (E. J. Mackrill).

52. Second-winter **Grey-headed Gull** *L. cirrocephalus*, South Africa, February 1974 (J. C. Sinclair)

53. Second-summer **Grey-headed gull** *L. cirrocephalus*, Kenya, July 1976 (T. Källqvist).

54. Adult summer **Grey-headed Gull** *L. cirrocephalus*, Peru, June 1981 (E. J. Mackrill).

55. Adult summer **Grey-headed Gull** *L. cirrocephalus*, South Africa, June 1973 (Gerry Nicholls).

56, 57. Adult **Grey-headed Gull** *L. cirrocephalus*, moulting from summer to winter plumage, Peru, January 1981 (E. J. Mackrill).

58. Adult summer **Grey-headed Gull** *L. cirrocephalus*, Kenya, July 1976 (T. Källqvist).

59. **Grey-headed Gulls** *L. cirrocephalus*, including one first-winter (right), South Africa, August 1976 (Gerry Nicholls).

60, 61. Juvenile **Common Gull** *L. canus*, Netherlands, August 1980 (Dirk Moerbeek).

62. First-winter **Common Gull** *L. canus*, London, February 1979 (R. J. Chandler).

63. First-winter **Common Gull** *L. canus*, Humberside, January 1971 (Richard Vaughan).

64. First-winter **Common Gulls** *L. canus*, Kent, March 1976 (Pamela Harrison).

65, 66.   First-winter **Common Gull** *L. canus*, Finland, December 1978 (P. Puhjo).

67.   First-winter **Common Gull** *L. canus*, London, February 1979 (R. J. Chandler).

68.   First-summer **Common Gull** *L. canus*, Kent, April 1976 (Pamela Harrison).

69.   First-summer **Common Gull** *L. canus*, Merseyside, May 1981 (Peter M. Harris).

70. **Common Gull** *L. canus*, starting moult from first-summer to second-winter, Lincolnshire, June 1980 (E. J. Mackrill).

71. **Common Gull** *L. canus*, moulting from first-summer to second-winter, Netherlands, August 1980 (Dirk Mocrbeek).

72. Second-winter (front) and first-winter **Common Gulls** *L. canus*, London, February 1979 (R. J. Chandler).

73, 74.   Second-winter **Common Gull** *L. canus*, Co. Cork, October 1975 (Richard T. Mills).

75.   Second-winter (left) and adult winter **Common Gulls** *L. canus*, Humberside, November 1970 (Richard Vaughan).

76.   Adult winter **Common Gull** *L. canus*, Somerset, December 1974 (Wendy Dickson).

77. Adult summer **Common Gull** *L. canus*, Norway, July 1956 (John Barlee).

78. Adult summer **Common Gull** *L. canus*, Strathclyde, June 1976 (Pamela Harrison).

79, 80. First-winter **Mediterranean Gull** *L. melanocephalus*, Surrey, October 1978 (R. J. Chandler).

81. First-winter **Mediterranean Gull** *L. mela-nocephalus*, Surrey, December 1978 (R. J. Chandler).

82. First-winter **Mediterranean Gull** *L. mela-nocephalus*, Surrey, January 1979 (Alistair Forsyth).

83. First-winter **Mediterranean Gull** *L. melanocephalus*, Sussex, December 1963 (R. H. Charlwood).

84. First-winter **Mediterranean Gull** *L. melanocephalus* (left) with first-winter Black-headed Gull *L. ridibundus*, Sussex, December 1963 (R. H. Charlwood).

85. **Mediterranean Gull** *L. melanocephalus* near end of moult from first-summer to second-winter, Turkey, September 1976 (P. Puhjo).

86. Second-winter **Mediterranean Gull** *L. melanocephalus,* Belgium, September 1976 (P. Devillers).

87. **Mediterranean Gull** *L. melanocephalus* moulting from second-summer to third-winter/ adult winter, Cornwall, August 1968 (J. B. & S. Bottomley).

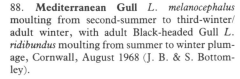

88. **Mediterranean Gull** *L. melanocephalus* moulting from second-summer to third-winter/ adult winter, with adult Black-headed Gull *L. ridibundus* moulting from summer to winter plumage, Cornwall, August 1968 (J. B. & S. Bottomley).

89.   Adult winter **Mediterranean Gull** *L. melanocephalus* with first-winter Black-headed Gull *L. ridibundus*, USSR, November 1976 (Pamela Harrison).

90.   Adult winter **Mediterranean** *L. melanocephalus* (right) and Black-headed Gull *L. ridibundus*, Kent, autumn 1964 (Pamela Harrison).

91.   Adult **Mediterranean Gull** *L. melanocephalus* near end of moult from winter to summer plumage, Surrey, February 1978 (R. J. Chandler).

92, 93.   Adult summer **Mediterranean Gulls** *L. melanocephalus*, Greece, May 1968. A comparison with Photo 91 demonstrates how the apparent extent of the hood on all hooded gulls can be affected by the posture of the individual: the more hunched the posture, the less extensive the hood (Wolfgang Makatsch).

94, 95, 96, 97. **Ring-billed Gulls** *L. delawarensis* near end of moult from juvenile to first-winter, USA, August 1980 (E. J. Mackrill).

98. **Ring-billed Gull** *L. delawarensis* near end of moult from juvenile to first-winter (note the few remaining dark-centred, juvenile scapulars), Canada, September 1979 (Philip Perry).

99. First-winter **Ring-billed Gull** *L. delawarensis*, USA, December 1975 (Robert Barber).

100, 101.   First-winter **Ring-billed Gulls** *L. delawarensis*, USA, October 1980 (E. J. Mackrill).

102.   First-winter **Ring-billed Gull** *L. delawarensis*, USA, February 1974 (Davis Finch).

103. **Ring-billed Gull** *L. delawarensis* moulting from first-winter to first-summer, USA, April 1977 (Jean Terschuren).

104. First-summer **Ring-billed Gull** *L. delawarensis*, USA, April 1977 (Jean Terschuren).

105. First-summer **Ring-billed Gull** *L. delawarensis*, Merseyside, May 1981. The missing innermost one or two primaries indicates the start of the moult to second-winter, which apparently takes place on average a month earlier than on Common Gull *L. canus* (Peter M. Harris).

106. Second-winter **Ring-billed Gull** *L. Delawarensis*, Cornwall, February 1979 (W. R. Hirst).

107. Second-winter **Ring-billed Gull** *L. delawarensis*, USA, March 1976 (Roger Higson).

108.   Second-summer **Ring-billed Gull** *L. delawarensis*, Canada, June 1977 (John W. Chardine).

109.   Adult winter **Ring-billed Gull** *L. delawarensis*, USA, March 1976 (Roger Higson).

110. Adult summer **Ring-billed Gulls** *L. delawarensis*, Canada, June 1977 (John W. Chardine).

111. Adult summer **Ring-billed Gulls** *L. delawarensis*, USA, March 1968 (P. Devillers).

112.   Juvenile **Laughing Gull** *L. atricilla*, USA, September 1980 (Leif Schack-Nielsen).

113.   Juvenile **Laughing Gull** *L. atricilla*, USA, August 1976 (Alan Brady).

114.   **Laughing Gull** *L. atricilla* moulting from juvenile to first-winter, USA, September 1980 (Leif Schack-Nielsen).

115. First-winter **Laughing Gull** *L. atricilla*, USA, October 1978 (J. B. & S. Bottomley).

116. First-winter **Laughing Gull** *L. atricilla*, USA, October 1980 (E. J. Mackrill).

117. First-winter **Laughing Gull** *L. atricilla*, Dorset, April 1969 (J. B. & S. Bottomley).

118. First-winter **Laughing Gull** *L. atricilla*, Dorset, April 1969 (J. B. & S. Bottomley).

119. First-summer **Laughing Gull** *L. atricilla*, USA, April 1980 (S. R. D. da Prato).

120. Second-winter **Laughing Gull** *L. atricilla*, USA, April 1980 (E. J. Mackrill).

121. Second-winter **Laughing Gull** *L. atricilla*, USA, April 1980 (E. J. Mackrill).

122. Second-winter **Laughing Gull** *L. atricilla*, Dumfries & Galloway, October 1978 (Donald A. Smith).

123. First-winter, second-winter and adult winter **Laughing Gulls** *L. atricilla*, USA, October 1978 (J. B. & S. Bottomley).

124.   Adult **Laughing Gull** *L. atricilla* moulting from summer to winter plumage (one new, white-tipped primary is visible, the remainder are old), USA, October 1978 (J. B. & S. Bottomley).

125.   Adult **Laughing Gull** *L. atricilla* moulting from summer to winter plumage (outermost primaries only partially grown), USA, October 1980 (E. J. Mackrill).

126.   Adult summer **Laughing Gull** *L. atricilla*, USA, July 1977 (Alan Brady).

127, 128.   Adult summer **Laughing Gulls** *L. atricilla*, USA, July 1980 (E. J. Mackrill).

129.   Adult summer **Laughing Gull** *L. atricilla*,
USA, July 1980 (E. J. Mackrill).

130.   Adult summer **Laughing Gull** *L. atricilla*,
USA, summer 1978 (E. J. Mackrill).

131. **Franklin's Gull** *L. pipixcan* near end of moult from juvenile to first-winter, Canada, September 1979 (Philip Perry).

132. First-winter **Franklin's Gull** *L. pipixcan*, Galapagos, December 1976 (Norman van Swelm).

133. First-winter **Franklin's Gulls** *L. pipixcan*, Peru, November 1980 (Arnoud B. van den Berg).

134, 135, 136. First-winter **Franklin's Gulls** *L. pipixcan*, Peru, November 1980 (E. J. Mackrill).

137. **Franklin's Gull** *L. pipixcan* showing (in this and in Photos 138 to 145) the progression of the complete spring moult from first-winter to first-summer, Peru, April 1981 (E. J. Mackrill).

138 to 145. (above and facing page) **Franklin's Gull** *L. pipixcan* showing (in these and with Photo 137) the progression of the complete spring moult from first-winter to first-summer. 138. Peru, March 1980 (Piet Meeth); 139, 140. Peru, April 1981 (E. J. Mackrill); 141. Peru, March 1981 (E. J. Mackrill); 142, 143, 144. Peru, April 1981 (E. J. Mackrill); 145. Peru, April 1981 (Moult to first-summer completed) (E. J. Mackrill).

146.   First-summer **Franklin's Gull** *L. pipixcan*, Chile, May 1980 (Arnoud B. van den Berg).

147. **Franklin's Gull** *L. pipixcan* near end of complete autumn moult (outer primaries not yet fully grown) from first-summer to second-winter (age indicated by large extent of black on wing-tip and small white primary tips), North Dakota, USA, August 1980 (E. J. Mackrill).

148.   Second-winter **Franklin's Gull** *L. pipixcan*, Peru, October 1980 (E. J. Mackrill).

150.   Second-winter **Franklin's Gull** *L. pipixcan*, Suffolk, February 1978 (M. Parker).

149.   Second-winter or adult winter **Franklin's Gull** *L. pipixcan*, Peru, November 1980. The intermediate wing-tip pattern renders firm age-diagnosis inadvisable (E. J. Mackrill).

151. **Franklin's Gull** *L. pipixcan* moulting from second-winter to second-summer, Peru, April 1981 (E. J. Mackrill).

152. Second-summer **Franklin's Gull** *L. pipixcan*, Peru, April 1981 (E. J. Mackrill).

153. Adult winter **Franklin's Gull** *L. pipixcan*, Peru, December 1975 (Piet Meeth).

154. Adult **Franklin's Gull** *L. pipixcan* in complete spring moult from winter to summer plumage, Peru, March 1980 (Piet Meeth).

155, 156, 157. Adult summer **Franklin's Gulls** *L. pipixcan*, Peru, April 1981 (E. J. Mackrill).

158, 159. Juvenile **Audouin's Gull** *L. audouinii*, Greece, August 1976 (Richard Vaughan).

160, 161. First-summer **Audouin's Gull** *L. audouinii*, Spain, April 1977 (Donald A. Smith).

162. Second-winter **Audouin's Gull** *L. audouinii*, Spain, September 1968 (F. G. H. Allen).

163. **Audouin's Gull** *L. audouinii*, Spain, April 1978. Obvious dark markings on the greater primary coverts indicate third-year plumage (D. Smallshire).

164. **Audouin's Gull** *L. audouinii*, probably third-summer (as indicated by the obvious dark marks on the greater primary coverts), Spain, April 1977 (Donald A. Smith).

165 Adult summer **Audouin's Gull** *L. audouinii*, Greece, May 1966 (Ilse Makatsch).

166.   Adult summer **Audouin's Gull** *L. audouinii*, Greece, May 1966 (Ilse Makatsch).

167.   Adult summer **Audouin's Gull** *L. audouinii*, Spain, April 1978 (D. Smallshire).

168, 169.   Adult summer **Audouin's Gull** *L. audouinii*, Spain, April 1980 (R. J. Chandler).

170.   Juvenile **Herring Gull** *L. argentatus*, Gwynedd, August 1980 (R. J. Chandler).

171.   Juvenile **Herring Gull** *L. argentatus*, Highland, August 1975 (R. J. Chandler).

172. Juvenile **Herring Gull** *L. argentatus*, Sweden, August 1976 (Stellan Hedgren).

173, 174. Juvenile **Herring Gull** *L. argentatus mongolicus*, Mongolia, August 1979 (Alan Kitson).

175. First-summer **Herring Gull** *L. argentatus*, North Yorkshire, May 1979 (R. J. Chandler).

176. First-summer **Herring Gull** *L. argentatus*, North Yorkshire, May 1979. The missing innermost primaries indicate the start of the moult to second-winter (R. J. Chandler).

177. Second-winter **Herring Gull** *L. argentatus*, Lothian, December 1980 (S. R. D. da Prato).

178.   Second-winter **Herring Gull** *L. argentatus*, North Humberside, March 1966 (Richard Vaughan).

180.   Second-summer **Herring Gull** *L. argenta-tus*, Gwynedd, April 1978 (R. J. Chandler).

179.   Second-summer **Herring Gull** *L. argenta-tus*, Gwynedd, April 1977 (R. J. Chandler).

181.　Second-summer **Herring Gull** *L. argentatus*, Gwynedd, April 1979 (R. J. Chandler).

182.　**Herring Gull** *L. argentatus* moulting from second-summer to third-winter, Merseyside, June 1981 (Peter M. Harris).

183.　**Herring Gull** *L. argentatus* moulting from second-summer to third-winter, Isle of Man, August 1981 (Peter M. Harris).

184. **Herring Gull** *L. argentatus* moulting from second-summer to third-winter, Isle of Man, August 1981 (Peter M. Harris).

185. Third-winter (or possibly an advanced individual in second-winter plumage) **Herring Gull** *L. argentatus*, London, January 1979 (R. J. Chandler).

186. Third-winter (or possibly an advanced individual in second-winter plumage) **Herring Gull** *L. argentatus*, London, January 1979 (R. J. Chandler).

187. Third-winter type **Herring Gull** *L. argentatus*, Finland, December 1978 (P. Puhjo).

188. Third-summer type **Herring Gull** *L. argentatus*, Gwynedd, April 1979 (R. J. Chandler).

189. Third-summer type (left) and adult summer **Herring Gulls** *L. argentatus*, Isle of Man, May 1976 (Pamela Harrison).

190. Third-summer type **Herring Gull** *L. argentatus michahellis*, Spain, April 1980 (R. J. Chandler).

191. Third-summer type **Herring Gull** *L. argentatus*, Isle of Man, May 1976 (Pamela Harrison).

192. Adult summer **Herring Gull** *L. argentatus*, Gwynedd, April 1979. Restricted dark markings on the greater primary coverts may be shown by individuals at any age, and are not necessarily a sign of immaturity (R. J. Chandler).

193. Adult winter **Herring Gulls** *L. argentatus*, North Humberside, December 1970 (Richard Vaughan)

194.   Adult summer **Herring Gulls** *L. argentatus*, Isle of Man, May 1976. Mainly with large species, it is often possible to distinguish between the sexes when a pair is standing together: here, the slightly larger general size and larger bill of the individual at the rear indicates that it is the male (Pamela Harrison).

195.   Adult summer **Herring Gull** *L. argentatus*, Co. Wexford, June 1974 (Richard T. Mills).

196. Adult summer and one second-summer (right) **Herring Gulls** *L. argentatus*, Scilly, April 1968 (John Barlee).

197. Adult summer **Herring Gulls** *L. argentatus atlantis*, Madeira, March 1980 (Arnoud B. van den Berg).

198, 199.   Adult summer **Herring Gulls** *L. argentatus michahellis*, Italy, March 1981
(R. J. Chandler).

200. Juvenile and adult summer **Lesser Black-backed Gull** *L. fuscus graellsii*, Dyfed, August 1977 (Richard Vaughan).

201. Juvenile **Lesser Black-backed Gull** *L. fuscus*, Kent, August 1976 (Pamela Harrison).

202. Juvenile **Lesser Black-backed Gull** *L. fuscus*, Kent, August 1976 (Pamela Harrison).

203, 204. Juvenile **Lesser Black-backed Gull** *L. fuscus fuscus*, Sweden, September 1976 (Stellan Hedgren).

205. **Lesser Black-backed Gulls** *L. fuscus*, Kent, August 1976. Near end of moult from first-summer to second-winter, probably *L. f. graellsii* on paleness of grey upperparts (centre); adult summer (left) and third-summer type (right) presumably *L. f. intermedius* on upperparts colour (Pamela Harrison).

212.   Adult summer **Lesser Black-backed Gull** *L. fuscus*, Norway, July 1956 (John Barlee).

213.   Adult summer **Lesser Black-backed Gull** *L. fuscus intermedius*, Norway, June 1976 (H. B. Skjelstad).

214, 215, 216, 217. Adult summer **Lesser Black-backed Gulls** *L. fuscus fuscus*, Sweden, June 1981 (R. J. Chandler).

218. Juvenile and adult summer **Great Black-backed Gulls** *L. marinus*, Gwynedd, August 1976 (R. J. Chandler).

219. First-winter **Great Black-backed Gull** *L. marinus*, North Humberside, January 1971 (Richard Vaughan).

220.   First-winter **Great Black-backed Gull** *L. marinus* (left) with third-winter type Herring Gull *L. argentatus* (right) and two first-winter Herring Gulls, Kent, October 1976 (Pamela Harrison).

221.   First-winter **Great Black-backed Gull** *L. marinus*, Lothian, January 1981 (S. R. D. da Prato).

222, 223. First-summer **Great Black-backed Gull** *L. marinus*, North Yorkshire, May 1979 (R. J. Chandler).

224. First-summer **Great Black-backed Gull** *L. marinus*, Merseyside, May 1981 (Peter M. Harris).

225. First-summer (left) and second-summer **Great Black-backed Gulls** *L. marinus*, North Yorkshire, May 1979 (R. J. Chandler).

226, 227. **Great Black-backed Gulls** *L. marinus* moulting
from first-summer to second-winter, Isle of Man, August 1981
(Peter M. Harris).

228. **Great Black-backed Gull** *L. marinus* moulting from first-summer to second-winter, Lincolnshire, June 1980 (E. J. Mackrill).

229. Second-winter **Great Black-backed Gull** *L. marinus*, Lothian, December 1980 (S. R. D. da Prato).

230. Second-summer **Great Black-backed Gull** *L. marinus*, North Yorkshire, May 1980 (R. J. Chandler).

231. Second-summer **Great Black-backed Gull**
L. marinus starting moult to third-winter, Dorset,
May 1980 (Peter M. Harris).

232. Second-summer **Great Black-backed Gull**
L. marinus starting moult to third-winter, Isle of
Man, May 1976 (Pamela Harrison).

233. **Great Black-backed Gull** *L. marinus*
moulting from second-summer to third-winter,
Lincolnshire, June 1980 (E. J. Mackrill).

234. Third-summer type **Great Black-backed Gull** *L. marinus* with first-winter Black-headed Gull *L. ridibundus* (left) and two adults moulting from winter to summer plumage, Humberside, February 1969 (Richard Vaughan).

235, 236. Third-summer type **Great Black-backed Gulls** *L. marinus*, North Yorkshire, May 1979. One has lost the innermost primary, indicating the start of moult to adult winter/fourth-winter (R. J. Chandler).

237. Third-summer type **Great Black-backed Gull** *L. marinus* moulting to adult winter/fourth-winter, Norfolk, August 1977 (R. J. Chandler).

238.   Adult summer **Great Black-backed Gulls** *L. marinus* with first-summer Herring Gull *L. argentatus*, Isle of Man, May 1976 (Pamela Harrison).

239.   Adult **Great Black-backed Gull** *L. marinus* moulting from summer to winter plumage, Norfolk, August 1977 (R. J. Chandler).

240. Juvenile **Great Black-headed Gull** *L. ichthyaetus*, Mongolia, August 1979 (Alan Kitson).

241. First-winter **Great Black-headed Gull** *L. ichthyaetus* with first-winter and adult Sooty Gulls *L. hemprichii*, Kenya, February 1974 (the first record of Great Black-headed Gull in Kenya) (P. L. Britton).

242. First-winter **Great Black-headed Gull** *L. ichthyaetus*, Bahrain, February 1979 (P. D. Goriup).

243, 244, 245. First-summer **Great Black-headed Gull** *L. ichthyaetus*, Mongolia, May 1977 (Alan Kitson)

246, 247.   First-summer starting moult to second-winter and adult summer **Great Black-headed Gulls** *L. ichthyaetus*, USSR, May 1978 (E. N. Panov).

248. First-summer **Great Black-headed Gull** *L. ichthyaetus*, USSR, April 1974 (V. A. Zubakin).

249, 250. Second-winter **Great Black-headed Gull** *L. ichthyaetus* near end of moult from first summer, captive, National Zoological Gardens, Abu Dhabi, December 1976 (Jeffery Boswall).

251, 252. Second-winter **Great Black-headed Gull** *L. ichthyaetus*, India, March 1978 (T. Shiota).

253, 254. Third-summer **Great Black-headed Gulls** *L. ichthyaetus*, Mongolia, May 1977 (Alan Kitson).

255, 256. Adult summer **Great Black-headed Gulls** *L. ichthyaetus*, USSR, May 1974 (V. A. Zubakin).

257, 258.   Adult summer **Great Black-headed Gulls** *L. ichthyaetus*, USSR, May 1974 (V. A. Zubakin).

259.   Adult summer **Great Black-headed Gulls** *L. ichthyaetus*, USSR, May 1978 (E. N. Panov).

260.   Adult summer **Great Black-headed Gulls** *L. ichthyaetus*, USSR, May (E. A. Bragin).

261. **Little Gull** *L. minutus* starting moult from juvenile to first-winter, North Humberside, September 1970 (Richard Vaughan).

262. First-winter **Little Gull** *L. minutus*, West Germany, May 1979 (Peter Gloe).

263. **Little Gull** *L. minutus* moulting from first-winter to first-summer, Cornwall, April 1971 (J. B. & S. Bottomley).

264. First-summer (centre) and second-summer or adult summer **Little Gulls** *L. minutus* with first-summer Black-headed Gull *L. ridibundus*, Lincolnshire, June 1973 (Keith Atkin).

265. First-summer **Little Gull** *L. minutus*, Poland, June 1980 (J. De Ridder).

266. **Little Gull** *L. minutus* moulting from first-summer to second-winter, Humberside, September 1980 (Philip Perry).

267. **Little Gull** *L. minutus* near end of moult from first-summer to second-winter (note remaining black-tipped, first-year tail feather, and that not all second-years have obvious black on the wing-tip), Humberside, September 1970 (Richard Vaughan).

268.   Second-winter **Little Gull** *L. minutus*, Humberside, September 1980 (Philip Perry).

269.   Second-winter **Little Gull** *L. minutus*, West Germany, August 1979. Few second-years have such obvious dark marks on the tertials (Peter Gloe).

270.   **Little Gull** *L. minutus*, Cornwall, March 1969. The whitish underwing-coverts suggest second-winter rather than adult winter plumage (J. B. & S. Bottomley).

271.   **Little Gull** *L. minutus* moulting from second-winter to second-summer, West Germany, May 1980 (Peter Gloe).

272. Second-summer **Little Gull** *L. minutus*, West Germany, May 1979 (Peter Gloe).

273. Second-summer **Little Gull** *L. minutus*, Poland, June 1980 (J. De Ridder).

274. Adult summer **Little Gull** *L. minutus*, Denmark, May 1958 (J. B. & S. Bottomley).

275. Adult summer **Little Gull** *L. minutus*, Poland, June 1980 (J. De Ridder).

276, 277, 278, 279. First-winter and adult-winter **Ross's Gulls** *R. rosea*, Japan, January 1974 (S. Mori).

280.   First-summer **Ross's Gull** *R. rosea*, Hampshire, July 1974 (J. B. & S. Bottomley).

281.   Adult winter **Ross's Gull** *R. rosea*, North Yorkshire, March 1976 (J. Seaviour).

282.   Adult winter **Ross's Gull** *R. rosea*, Shetland, January 1975 (Dennis Coutts).

283.   Adult summer **Ross's Gull** *R. rosea*, USSR, June 1978 (V. A. Zubakin).

285. Adult summer **Ross's Gull** *R. rosea*, USSR, June 1972 (P. Tomkovitch).

284. Adult summer **Ross's Gulls** *R. rosea*, USSR, July 1971 (A. A. Kistchinski).

286, 287. Adult summer **Ross's Gull** *R. rosea*, USSR, July 1972 (A. A. Kistchinski).

288, 289, 290. Juvenile **Sabine's Gull** *L. sabini*, Sweden, October 1969 (Bengt Bengtsson).

291, 292. First-winter **Sabine's Gulls** *L. sabini* moulting to first-summer, El Salvador, March 1980 (Piet Meeth).

293, 294. First-summer **Sabine's Gull** *L. sabini*, Lincolnshire, September 1974 (Keith Atkin).

295. Adult winter **Sabine's Gull** *L. sabini*, South Africa, February 1978 (J. C. Sinclair).

296. Adult **Sabine's Gull** *L. sabini* moulting from winter to summer plumage, El Salvador, March 1980 (Piet Meeth).

297. Adult **Sabine's Gull** *L. sabini* moulting from winter to summer plumage, South Africa, February 1979 (J. C. Sinclair).

298. Adult summer **Sabine's Gull** *L. sabini*, Canada, June 1976 (Brian Hawkes).

302. Juvenile **Kittiwake** *R. tridactyla*, Gwynedd, August 1979 (R. J. Chandler).

303. First-winter **Kittiwake** *R. tridactyla*, Lothian, February 1981 (S. R. D. da Prato).

304. First-summer **Kittiwake** *R. tridactyla*, North Yorkshire, May 1980 (R. J. Chandler).

305, 306.   First-summer **Kittiwake** *R. tridactyla*, Merseyside, June 1981 (Peter M. Harris).

307, 308.   First-summer **Kittiwakes** *R. tridactyla*, North Yorkshire, May 1979. The extreme wear and fading on some first-summer individuals is well shown, but the complete loss of the tail band on one is exceptional (R. J. Chandler).

309. First-summer **Kittiwake** *R. tridactyla*, Merseyside, June 1981 (Peter M. Harris).

310. Second-winter **Kittiwake** *R. tridactyla*, Ayrshire, January 1978 (Donald A. Smith).

311. Second-summer **Kittiwake** *R. tridactyla*, North Yorkshire, May 1980 (R. J. Chandler).

312. Second-summer **Kittiwake** *R. tridactyla*, Merseyside, June 1981 (Peter M. Harris).

313. Adult winter **Kittiwake** *R. tridactyla*, mid-Atlantic, winter 1969 (E. L. Marchant).

314. Adult summer **Kittiwake** *R. tridactyla*, North Yorkshire, May 1979 (R. J. Chandler).

315. Adult summer **Kittiwake** *R. tridactyla*, Isle of Man, May 1976 (Pamela Harrison).

316, 317. First-winter **Ivory Gull** *P. eburnea*, Belfast, December 1978 (A. McGeehan).

318. First-winter **Ivory Gull** *P. eburnea*, Northumberland, December 1979 (S. R. D. da Prato).

319, 320. First-winter **Ivory Gull** *P. ebur-nea*, Dorset, January 1980 (Jeff Pick).

321. First-summer **Ivory Gull** *P. eburnea*, Sweden, April 1971 (Stellan Hedgren).

322. Adult winter **Ivory Gull** *P. eburnea*, Shetland, December 1980 (Bobby Tulloch).

323. First-winter **Glaucous Gull** *L. hyperboreus*, Suffolk, January 1978 (Jeff Pick).

324. First-winter **Glaucous Gull** *L. hyperboreus*, Finland, January 1977 (J. Haapala).

325. First-winter **Glaucous Gull** *L. hyperboreus*, Finland, January 1977 (J. Haapala).

326. First-winter **Glaucous Gull** *L. hyperboreus*, Finland, February 1971 (M. Hario).

327. First-winter **Glaucous Gull** L. *hyperboreus*, Cornwall, February 1980. An exceptionally dark individual (W. R. Hirst).

328. First-winter or first-summer **Glaucous Gull** L. *hyperboreus*, Norway, February 1976 (H. B. Skjelstad).

329. First-summer **Glaucous Gull** *L. hyper-boreus*, Cornwall, February 1972 (J. B. & S. Bottomley).

330. First-summer **Glaucous Gull** *L. hyper-boreus*, with worn and faded wings and tail typical of this age, North Yorkshire, May 1980 (R. J. Chandler).

331. **Glaucous Gull** *L. hyperboreus* moulting from first-summer to second-winter, Strathclyde, July 1976 (Donald A. Smith).

332.   Second-winter **Glaucous Gull** *L. hyperboreus* (note pale iris), Strathclyde, January 1974 (Donald A. Smith).

333.   Second-winter **Glaucous Gull** *L. hyperboreus*, Co. Cork, January 1976 (Richard T. Mills).

334. Second-summer (left) and first-summer **Glaucous Gulls** *L. hyperboreus*, Iceland, June 1979 (R. N. Hobbs).

335. Second-summer **Glaucous Gull** *L. hyperboreus*, Cornwall, April 1972 (J. B. & S. Bottomley).

336. **Glaucous Gull** *L. hyperboreus* starting moult from second-summer to third-winter, Norway, April 1976 (H. B. Skjelstad).

337. **Glaucous Gull** *L. hyperboreus* starting moult from second-summer to third-
winter, Norway, April 1976 (H. B. Skjelstad).

338, 339. Third-winter **Glaucous Gull** *L. hyperboreus*
(the same individual as in Photos 336 and 337), Norway,
October 1976 (H. B. Skjelstad).

340. Third-summer **Glaucous Gull** *L. hyper-boreus*, Iceland, June 1974 (Jeffery Boswall).

341. Adult winter **Glaucous Gull** *L. hyper-boreus*, Lothian, winter 1978/79 (S. R. D. da Prato).

342. **Glaucous Gull** *L. hyperboreus*, probably fourth-summer (patchiness of grey upperparts and wing-coverts indicates that this individual is not fully mature), Cornwall, March 1974 (J. B. & S. Bottomley).

343. Adult summer **Glaucous Gull** *L. hyperboreus*, Iceland, June 1979 (R. N. Hobbs).

344. Juvenile **Iceland Gull** *L. glaucoides*, Greenland, August 1970 (Erik Isakson).

345. First-winter **Iceland Gull** *L. glaucoides* with two first-winter Herring Gulls *L. argentatus*, Netherlands, January 1976 (J. G. Prins).

346.   First-winter **Iceland Gull** *L. glaucoides*, Lothian, January 1981 (S. R. D. da Prato).

347.   First-winter **Iceland Gull** *L. glaucoides* with adult winter Black-headed Gulls *L. ridibundus*, Suffolk, January 1978 (Mike Parker).

348.   First-winter **Iceland Gull** *L. glaucoides*, Denmark, January 1965 (Jan Kihlmän).

349.   **Iceland Gull** *L. glaucoides* moulting from first-summer to second-winter, Scilly, September 1974. The timing of this individual's moult seems exceptionally late (resulting in extremely worn and faded tail feathers, primaries, greater coverts and lower scapulars), perhaps the result of some physical abnormality. The view has been expressed, however, that these anomalies, the coarse barring on the new coverts and scapulars, and the head/bill structure (but note that the head shape is affected by loose, moulting nape feathers) could be characters of an albinistic or leucistic Herring Gull *L. argentatus* (J. B. & S. Bottomley).

350, 351.   Second-winter **Iceland Gull** *L. glaucoides*, Sweden, February 1972 (Bengt Bensson).

352. **Iceland Gull** *L. glaucoides*, Netherlands, February 1981. The extensive clear grey on the upperparts and lesser and median coverts, and the generally whitish with uniform (rather than barred) pale brown markings on the wings and tail indicate third-year plumage, and this age-diagnosis is favoured by the author. IJzendoorn & Oreel (Dutch Birding 3:13–15), however, age it as a second-year because of the extensive blackish on the bill-tip, the yellowish-green bill-base, and the extensive brown on the wings and tail. It could well be an individual in 'advanced' second-year plumage, but it seems best to leave its age intermediate, at least until the variations of second- and third-year plumages of the Iceland Gull are better known (Dick Moerbeek).

353, 354. **Iceland Gull** *L. glaucoides*—details as Photo 352 (J. De Ridder).

355.   **Iceland Gull** L. glaucoides—details as Photo 352 (Edward van IJzendoorn).

356.   Adult summer **Iceland Gull** L. glaucoides, Lothian, March 1977 (S. R. D. & S. da Prato).

357, 358.   Juvenile **Sooty Gulls** *L. hemprichii*, Kenya, January 1977 (J. F. Reynolds).

359.   Three first-winter (right) and one adult or second-winter (left) **Sooty Gulls** *L. hemprichii*, Kenya, winter 1977 (P. L. Britton).

360. First-winter (right) and second-winter **Sooty Gulls** *L. hemprichii*, Kenya, January 1978 (Norman van Swelm).

361, 362. **Sooty Gulls** *L. hemprichii* moulting from first-summer to second-winter (note remaining, faded, first-year wing-coverts and pointed outer primaries), Yemen, April 1979 (R. F. Porter).

363. **Sooty Gull** *L. hemprichii* near end of moult from first-summer to second-winter, Yemen, April 1979 (R. F. Porter).

364. Second-year (left) and adult moulting from summer to winter **Sooty Gulls** *L. hemprichii*, Yemen, April 1979 (R. F. Porter).

365.   Second-year **Sooty Gull** *L. hemprichii* (note trace of age-diagnostic partial tail-band), Oman, October 1976 (M. D. Gallagher).

366.   Second-summer **Sooty Gull** *L. hemprichii*, Oman, July 1977 (M. D. Gallagher).

367.   Adult **Sooty Gull** *L. hemprichii* near end of moult from summer to winter plumage, Kenya, January 1978 (Norman van Swelm).

368. Adult summer **Sooty Gull** *L. hemprichii*, Oman, July 1977 (M. D. Gallagher).

369.   Adult **Sooty Gull** *L. hemprichii*, Oman, October 1976 (M. D. Gallagher).

370. Two immature, probably first-winter (centre) and adult summer **White-eyed Gulls** *L. leucopthalmus*, Egypt, March 1980 (Jan Visser).

371. **White-eyed Gull** *L. leucopthalmus* moulting from first-summer to second-winter, Egypt, September 1980 (Wim C. Mullié).

372. Second-summer **White-eyed Gull** *L. leucopthalmus*, Yemen, April 1980. The bill on this individual is wholly blackish, and the greater coverts and coverts of outer wing brownish. The broad, blackish secondary bar, and relatively narrow white trailing edge and small white tips on inner primaries indicate second-year rather than fully adult plumage (compare Photo 375) (S. C. Madge).

373. Three second-summer or adult summer **White-eyed Gulls** *L. leucopthalmus* moulting to winter plumage, and two Sooty Gulls *L. hemprichii* (foreground and right), Yemen, April 1979 (R. F. Porter).

374.   Adult summer **White-eyed Gull** *L. leucop-thalmus* (left) and two adult summer Sooty Gulls *L. hemprichii*, Yemen, April 1979 (R. F. Porter).

375, 376.   Adult summer **White-eyed Gulls** *L. leucopthalmus*, Yemen, April 1980 (S. D. G. Cook).